THE NEXT GOLD RUSH

To Nina,

I hope you enjoy
reading my book!
Glad we connected :)

Ethan Turer

THE NEXT GOLD RUSH

THE FUTURE OF INVESTING
IN PEOPLE

ETHAN TURER

NEW DEGREE PRESS

THE NEXT GOLD RUSH

The Future of Investing in People

ISBN   978-1-63676-494-8   *Paperback*

978-1-63730-411-2   *Kindle Ebook*

978-1-63730-412-9   *Ebook*

To my mom, for being my #1 supporter, fan, and for always believing in me. Thank you for encouraging me throughout my author journey.

Contents

———

PART 1   **CRYPTO-CURIOUS** **9**

INTRODUCTION: MY BIG IDEA 11

CHAPTER 1   BITCOIN, ETHEREUM, AND CHALLENGE COIN 19

CHAPTER 2   MONEY, FIAT CURRENCY, AND
CRYPTOCURRENCY 33

CHAPTER 3   BUBBLES: BUILD, BURST, REPEAT 45

CHAPTER 4   DEBT: TRAP OR TOOL?. 57

PART 2   **CRYPTO-CONSCIOUS** **71**

CHAPTER 5   MONEY IN POLITICS. 73

CHAPTER 6   ENTREPRENEURSHIP AND RAISING MONEY .85

CHAPTER 7   INFLUENCERS AND FOLLOWERS 97

CHAPTER 8   YOUR COIN: THE LIFE CYCLE. 111

PART 3   **CRYPTO-CAPITALIST** **129**

CHAPTER 9   WARNING: IT'S THE WILD WEST 131

CHAPTER 10   INVESTING IN CRYPTO. 145

CHAPTER 11   EVOLUTION OF PUBLIC OFFERINGS 169

CHAPTER 12   THE NEXT GOLD RUSH. 183

CONCLUSION: TL;DR. 211

ACKNOWLEDGEMENTS. 219

BIBLIOGRAPHY 223

ABOUT THE AUTHOR. 253

PART 1

CRYPTO-CURIOUS

My Big Idea

On Saturday, May 5, 2018, (a.k.a. Cinco de Mayo) I was in attendance at the second annual Cal Poly Entrepreneurs (CPE) Officer Alumni Reunion. After serving two years on the board of the Cal Poly Entrepreneurs Club—"The best club on campus" according to Cal Poly President Jeffrey Armstrong—I was attending my first alumni event ever. I remember this weekend and that event as the spark of my big idea and the subsequent motivation for writing this book.

Some background on me and why this event was the perfect catalyst for my journey as an entrepreneur. First, I graduated from Cal Poly San Luis Obispo (SLO) in May 2018 with a degree in business entrepreneurship. My love for entrepreneurship came from the Cal Poly Entrepreneurs Club. We were a bunch of misfits who all had one thing in common: an entrepreneurial mindset. We worked hard and played harder. Nothing compares to the rush of taking an idea and making it a reality. I did this by organizing the first ever Officer Alumni Reunion, where we brought back officers from the club's founding, eight years prior. We reminisced about the past and showed how the club had progressed in those eight years. It was so successful that this event turned into an annual tradition for officer alumni to return to San Luis Obispo and reconnect with old friends and make some new ones as well.

The second annual CPE Reunion started in the morning with a hike up Bishop's Peak, the most popular hiking spot in town. I recall talking excitedly about the startup I was interning for, Unanimous AI. They had a unique approach to gathering the intelligence of groups using their software. People would collectively answer questions in real-time using Unanimous AI's swarm technology. This was also the first company I worked for after graduation, so my enthusiasm was at an all-time high. I was put in charge of a cryptocurrency project where we attempted to predict the prices of Bitcoin, Ethereum, and other cryptocurrencies. The results were inconclusive, but at the time, the prospect of being able to predict prices of a very volatile market was exhilarating.

Later that evening, the alumni group reconvened at The Hothouse, a startup incubator, in downtown SLO. We ate food and talked about the glory days of being a CPE officer. Once we were done swapping funny stories about college, I made a toast to my close friend Brett Beer Tyler, who had passed away in October 2017. He was CPE's VP of marketing, and he was a marketing genius, constantly ideating and pushing the boundaries of what was possible. Brett, a.k.a. the Pundit, was repeatedly making people laugh with his puns. Many people would recall that their first exposure to CPE was through Brett and his genuinely remarkable personality. This was the tearjerker part of the event, but he is one of my inspirations for writing this book, as I aspire to be like him and honor his memory.

Brett will always hold a special place in my heart and nothing I say will ever truly do justice to the impact he had on everyone around him. After that emotional moment, we continued the festivities with a Mediterranean-style dinner. Now this is where the fun started. Our group moved across the street to The Lofts, which was a new entrepreneurial housing community with an outdoor patio for large gatherings. There was mingling, games, interesting conversations, and networking. Imagine being around thirty inspirational people who were the next PayPal Mafia (Thiel and Masters, 2014), having fun and creating the future, all in one night.

That's when I had my big idea for *The Next Gold Rush*. There must be a way to support the next generation of entrepreneurs with cryptocurrency. What if there was a way to invest in the person behind the startup? If there was a coin tied to the value of the entrepreneur, then that would take most of the risk out of the investment since most entrepreneurs continue creating, even after their first startup fails. All these ideas came to me at once, and it felt like a lightning strike to the skull. I started pitching my new idea to some of the alumni and got them curiously excited about it too.

Since that moment, when I had my epiphany, I've continued to research and explore the world of cryptocurrency. My idea has become increasingly refined and even more ambitious. I want to create a cryptocurrency that will allow every person to have their own coin connected to their worth. Currently, the richest people are evaluated by *Forbes* in their "richest people in the world" segment, based on the assets they have accumulated (Dolan, 2021). What about the rest of us? Do we want to compare each other based on everyone's respective accumulation of wealth? If we had a method of evaluating people other than using money, wealth, profits, and stock gains, then we would be one step closer to living in a better world.

I am an early-stage entrepreneur with little to no assets and no previous experience running a company. It would be very hard, almost impossible, to find an investor who would invest in my first startup, which is statistically likely to fail (Kotashev and Cerdeira, 2021). If I instead created Ethan Coin and asked investors to buy my coin to fund the startup, then even if the first startup fails, Ethan Coin isn't a failure. Those same investors would already be invested, via Ethan Coin, in the next company I start. Even if I do not create another company, I will still find ways to improve my quality of life over time. That's how Ethan Coin measures value. Not just monetary quality but immaterial things like hours volunteered, my number of followers online, my health, and so much more.

It is less risky for investors because people generally bounce back over the course of their lives. Another interesting concept is that I'm creating a new asset class. People can trade coins like investing in stocks in the stock market. Except instead of trading shares of companies you are investing in people's coins. If you think about it, what are companies except a collection of people? There are endless possibilities for how this idea can change society for the better, and I am excited to dive even deeper into those possibilities in this book.

This new economic system is limitless since every person can create their own coin, meaning that everyone may have their own mission for raising funds. The next gold rush is in cryptocurrency but it's not investing in Bitcoin, it's investing in people. People are the backbone of every society and human institution. We make up every community, company, government, organization, and country. Collectively, people are the global economy and have the power to shape the world. Creating a new economic system is no small feat, but it is an essential change that can lead to changing how we do everything.

The world's richest 1 percent have more than twice as much wealth as 6.9 billion people (Oxfam 2019). According to a report by the Federal Reserve, nearly 40 percent of Americans could not cover a $400 emergency expense. While the richest people in the world have benefited from our current economic systems, the rest of the world has been struggling. The rich are getting richer faster, and income inequality has been increasing every year (HOROWITZ, IGIELNIK, and KOCHHAR, 2020). Many more alarming statistics show the current state of our economy. We need to change things for the better, or they will only get worse.

The main problem we need to tackle is our economy. Think about the economy as a machine that tells people where to spend their time, captures all their economic value, and incentivizes behaviors across the world. The global economy is the core machine, which makes it the primary problem that needs to be solved. While lawmakers and economists work to reform our current economy, cryptocurrency offers a new vision for how people can interact with each other. The ability for people to invest in one another is a win-win for the global economy because we can all win given the right incentives and human systems.

I feel compelled to write this book because ideas can change the world. I had an idea in 2018—ten years after Bitcoin was created—for a new type of cryptocurrency, and ever since then, I have become more and more excited about a future where this idea becomes a reality. That's my motivation. I want to see this idea in the world so that we can all prosper. I am very passionate about solving problems, and my curiosity has led me to write a book geared toward doing just that: solving problems through cryptocurrency. I like to understand big picture concepts and see how all the puzzle pieces come together. As you read this book, I will do my best to show how cryptocurrency can change every aspect of our lives.

This book has three parts for three groups of people: Crypto-Curious, Crypto-Conscious, and Crypto-Capitalist. Each part builds on top of the previous one, but you can read it from start to finish or start in the section that applies to you. Crypto-Curious people are beginners. They may have heard of Bitcoin before, but that's about it. They are curious about cryptocurrency and want to learn more. Crypto-Conscious people already know some of the basics around cryptocurrency but are intrigued about how it might become more relevant and accessible to their lives. Crypto-Capitalists are people who want to invest more of their time, money, and resources into the cryptocurrency field. These people have a more advanced understanding of cryptocurrency and want to be a part of the next gold rush in cryptocurrency.

I hope that this book will inspire you about the future of cryptocurrency and all the possibilities for positive change going forward. Reading this book is the first step to understanding a new way of living in the modern world. I want you to start asking yourself how cryptocurrency could make a difference in the world and how you could help make that change. We need to empower a generation of changemakers and problem solvers if we are ever going to have a chance at living in a world that works for all of us, not just the wealthy and powerful. If you are reading this, then you are now part of that change, and we have a lot of work to do.

CHAPTER 1

Bitcoin, Ethereum, and Challenge Coin

SATOSHI NAKAMOTO AND BITCOIN

"[Bitcoin is] everything you don't understand about money combined with everything you don't understand about computers."

—JOHN OLIVER, HOST OF LAST WEEK
TONIGHT WITH JOHN OLIVER

To tell the story of Bitcoin, you must first understand that nobody knows who created it. The architect of Bitcoin used the alias "Satoshi Nakamoto," which could either be a person or a group of people. As of this writing, we still don't know their true identity. There are some things we do know about this mysterious founder, however (Feins 2017). We know that they released a white paper, or blueprint, explaining the technical aspects of Bitcoin and blockchain networks. Other than that, there's been little digital footprint from Satoshi Nakamoto, who would be one of the top one hundred richest people alive today if their identity was known. Satoshi owns over 1.1 million Bitcoins, and at a value of nearly $65,000 at its peak in April 2021, that's over $70 Billion (Phillips, 2021).

Let's take a step back and try to understand the significance of Bitcoin and why Satoshi Nakamoto has become one of the symbols of the cryptocurrency community. In 2008, the Bitcoin white paper titled "Bitcoin: A Peer-to-Peer Electronic Cash System" was published online, and a few months later, the source code was made available for anyone to use. Also happening around that time was the 2008 financial crash, which was a result of the housing market collapsing. This juxtaposition of events is one of the most symbolic, as the failure of one financial system led to the birth of another.

To understand why the housing market collapsed in 2008, you must also understand the role of banks, the Federal Reserve, and the US government. Here's a brief oversimplification of what happened: People who couldn't afford to buy homes were getting risky loans from banks. Those loans were then combined and packaged as an investment. That investment was considered not risky and was speculated on by other banks and financial institutions. This created a big bubble which left banks over-leveraged, meaning they couldn't afford to pay their losses. That's where the idea of banks being "too big to fail" comes in, because if they did fail, it would threaten to create a domino effect of financial collapses (Singh, 2020).

The role that the US government and Federal Reserve played was just as much a part of the problem. In order to save face, the US government bailed out the banks. The Wall Street bailout package was passed in October 2008. Basically, the government bought $700 billion worth of these bad mortgage investments to keep financial markets from collapsing further (Nolen, 2020).

Lastly, the Federal Reserve—America's Central Bank—responded by dropping interest rates to almost zero and implementing quantitative easing. Simply, dropping interest rates to almost nothing makes money cheaper and in theory leads to more spending and economic output. Quantitative easing means printing new money at the scale of trillions of dollars (Yglesias, 2014). Imagine being on a sinking ship and the captain orders you to pump air into the holes instead of patching them. He then orders you to continue pumping air to keep the failing boat from sinking further instead of making any modifications or chartering a new vessel.

I believe that Bitcoin's creation in the midst of all that was going on wasn't a coincidence. We needed an alternative, and we got it. Now that you know the significance of the timing of 2008, let's explore why Bitcoin is the better alternative.

Here's what Bitcoin is, straight from the source:

"A purely peer-to-peer version of electronic cash would allow online payments to be sent directly from one party to another without going through a financial institution" (Nakamoto, 2008).

Satoshi Nakamoto continues their Bitcoin abstraction by saying:

Digital signatures provide part of the solution, but the main benefits are lost if a trusted [centralized] third party is still required to prevent double-spending. We propose a solution to the double-spending problem using a peer-to-peer network. The network timestamps transactions by hashing them into an ongoing chain of hash-based proof-of-work, forming a record that cannot be changed without redoing the proof-of-work. The longest chain not only serves as proof of the sequence of events witnessed, but proof that it came from the largest pool of CPU power. As long as a majority of CPU power is controlled by nodes that are not cooperating to attack the network, they'll generate the longest chain and outpace attackers. The network itself requires minimal structure. Messages are broadcast on a best effort basis, and nodes can leave and rejoin the network at will, accepting the longest proof-of-work chain as proof of what happened while they were gone.

If you didn't understand the text above, then you're just like me when I first read it. I'm going to explain Bitcoin in parts to make it as clear and easily comprehendible as possible. I encourage all readers to explore these concepts further and read the whole Bitcoin white paper on your own. Go to Bitcoin.org to learn more.

The core accomplishment of Bitcoin is that there's no central authority controlling the transactions in the network. Banks usually act as the central authority verifying all transactions and taking fees for the privilege of storing your money with them. Bitcoin is able to do this by tracking transactions through a decentralized network (Martin, 2018a).

The terms "decentralized" and "peer-to-peer" are used interchangeably. Whereas banks and other clearinghouses process their transactions in a central location like a server farm, Bitcoin uses many separate nodes, or users' computers, to process every transaction. This peer-to-peer network verifies transactions in groups called blocks. Since the network is dispersed across many nodes around the world, there's no single point of failure, which makes Bitcoin almost impossible to shut down, manipulate, or control (Martin, 2018).

Every confirmed transaction is then connected in a chain of blocks, also known as a blockchain. Blockchain is the underlying technology that makes Bitcoin possible. Satoshi Nakamoto was the first to utilize blockchain technology, and Bitcoin was the first cryptocurrency to come from this breakthrough technology. The blockchain is designed to be an immutable ledger, meaning that once a block is added to the chain, it cannot be changed, thus making a permanent string of unchangeable transactions.

Another key innovation of Bitcoin is that it solves the double-spend problem. This is the problem that has made decentralized digital currencies previously impossible. How do you make sure that someone with a set amount of money does not send those funds more than once? Banks solve this problem through accounting or tracking via the Federal Reserve. Bitcoin solves the double-spend problem by having a vast network of mining nodes verify that the same Bitcoin was not spent twice (Chohan, 2021).

There is a network of nodes that validate blocks or transactions through mining. Mining is the process of running complex cryptographic algorithms until they are verified on the blockchain, and then Bitcoin is rewarded for adding a new block to the chain (Lai, 2018). Miners receive processing fees or "gas fees" for verifying Bitcoin transactions, which are relatively small compared to traditional financial institutions.

Let's look at this another way: Fiat money, or digital money, is already very common in today's society. Venmo has become a popular way to send money amongst friends. When someone sends their friend money, they aren't able to send more money than they have. Venmo has an internal database for tracking the transactions of all its users. This app works similarly to Bitcoin except instead of trusting the central authorities at Venmo to keep track of your money and transactions, you are trusting the blockchain technology and immutable ledger that's verified by a network of nodes.

To rehash, Bitcoin is a digital currency that is decentralized and can be trusted because of the blockchain technology that powers it, and it is not a central authority like a bank. Satoshi Nakamoto designed Bitcoin to act as an alternative to fiat currency, which is controlled by a central bank. Blockchain technology demonstrates that people can trust that they have the freedom outside the control of banks, governments, and other central authorities.

I'll end with this quote from the Founder and Chairman of the X Prize Foundation, Peter Diamandis:

"At its core, Bitcoin is a smart currency, designed by very forward-thinking engineers. It eliminates the need for banks, gets rid of credit card fees, currency exchange fees, money transfer fees, and reduces the need for lawyers in transitions...All good things" (Rosulek, 2017).

VITALIK BUTERIN AND ETHEREUM

Bitcoin is the godfather cryptocurrency which started it all, but Ethereum is the platform that makes cryptocurrencies more than just digital currency.

In 2013, five years after the creation of Bitcoin, Vitalik Buterin created Ethereum. Vitalik is a Russian-Canadian programmer, writer, and entrepreneur. He was born in Russia and moved to Canada at the age of six. Growing up, he excelled in all things computers and was recognized as a gifted student. His ability to learn new subjects well led to his groundbreaking achievement.

Vitalik's interest in Bitcoin came from his father back in 2011. His dad is a long-time programmer and startup founder. Vitalik believed that central authorities were responsible for many of society's ills. He said, "I had a much more cartoon mentality. I saw everything to do with either government regulation or corporate control as just being plain evil. And I assumed that people in those institutions were kind of like Mr. Burns, sitting behind their desks saying, 'Excellent. How can I screw a thousand people over this time'" (Peck, 2016).

Even though Vitalik's worldview changed over the years, he still held the core belief that the powerful, wealthy, and elite needed to be disempowered. He explained, "I think a large part of the consequence is necessarily going to be disempowering some of these centralized players to some extent because ultimately, power is a zero-sum game. And if you talk about empowering the little guy, as much as you want to couch it in flowery terminology that makes it sound fluffy and good, you are necessarily disempowering the big guy. And personally, I say screw the big guy. They have enough money already" (Peck, 2016).

Eventually, Vitalik wanted to dive deeper into the Bitcoin community and saw a job posting to write articles for *Bitcoin Weekly*, which paid five Bitcoins for each post. That was around $20 in Bitcoin back in 2011, which would be over $300,000 in 2020. That job led to Vitalik co-founding *Bitcoin Magazine*, where he contributed as the lead writer ("Who is Vitalik Buterin," 2021). Through his blockchain research, work, and travels, Vitalik realized that there was another opportunity for blockchain that could lead to limitless potential. The idea became Ethereum, which is the world's first fully programmable blockchain ("What is Ethereum?" 2021).

Blockchain is to Bitcoin what the internet is to email—a system on top of which you can build applications and programs (Martin 2018). Dmitry Buterin, co-founder of BlockGeeks and Vitalik's father, recommended the following analogy for this book: "Bitcoin is like a calculator (purpose built for specific functions); Ethereum is like a smartphone where you can install and run any app developed for it."

Vitalik published a white paper explaining Ethereum back in 2013 that said:

The intent of Ethereum is to create an alternative protocol for building decentralized applications, providing a different set of tradeoffs that we believe will be very useful for a large class of decentralized applications, with particular emphasis on situations where rapid development time, security for small and rarely used applications, and the ability of different applications to very efficiently interact, are important (Buterin, 2021).

Vitalik Buterin continues explaining that:

Ethereum does this by building what is essentially the ultimate abstract foundational layer: a blockchain with a built-in Turing-complete programming language, allowing anyone to write smart contracts and decentralized applications where they can create their own arbitrary rules for ownership, transaction formats and state transition functions.... Smart contracts, cryptographic 'boxes' that contain value and only unlock it if certain conditions are met, can also be built on top of the platform, with vastly more power than that offered by Bitcoin scripting because of the added powers of Turing-completeness, value-awareness, blockchain-awareness, and state.

Let's break this down like we did for Bitcoin. The main problem that Ethereum solves is that Bitcoin is only made for financial purposes like making payments, but many more things can be done with blockchain technology. One of the issues for people that wanted to venture away from Bitcoin's style of blockchain is that they had to start from scratch. That means they had to program all the aspects of Bitcoin that make it revolutionary before they could try to build their own cryptocurrency. Vitalik saw this glaring problem as an obstacle to mass adoption and decided that there could be an easier way (Casey, 2020).

People no longer need to build a blockchain from the ground up because Ethereum will allow users to build on top of their blockchain. It's like building a house where Ethereum laid the foundation, provided all the tools, and allowed its users to build whatever they want on top of it. The "whatever they want" that users are building is called a "decentralized application," or DApp for short. Around three thousand DApps exist within the Ethereum network, and that number is growing every day ("State of the DApps—DApp Statistics," 2021).

It may be hard to imagine what these DApps are based on the description above. Just as Vitalik theorized, the possibilities of blockchain technology are endless. The top ten categories of DApps in order from most to least popular—according to Stateofthedapps.com—include: finance, exchanges, security, wallet, development, games, social, governance, storage, property, media, identity.

The brilliant mind of Vitalik Buterin envisioned this future when he developed Ethereum. He saw the potential of building a foundational layer that was simple, universal, modular, agile, and non-discriminatory. Turing-completeness is a way of saying that the blockchain is more flexible compared to

Bitcoin, which is limited. Vitalik ensured that his blockchain would be Turing-complete so that there were many more capabilities for its users (Buterin, 2021).

There are two more breakthroughs that make Ethereum a game changer: smart contracts and the Ethereum Virtual Machine (EVM). Smart contracts are computer programs that execute terms of sophisticated contracts and control the outcomes of that contract. Smart contracts make transactions trackable, transparent, and permanent. Instead of allowing only currency to be tracked and maintained on a blockchain ledger, smart contracts allow computer code to be tracked and maintained on the ledger. This smart contract software layer, combined with Ethereum's blockchain foundational layer, makes the Ethereum Virtual Machine. EVM is the network of computers that acts as a supercomputer running all these transactions. Additionally, EVM ensures a separation between hosts and DApps in each software application (Casey, 2020).

Ethereum has evolved since its inception eight years ago, to Ethereum 2.0 (Millman, 2020). Ethereum's latest updates are designed to scale the network, so it can be more competitive with legacy payment networks (like Visa) that can process thousands of transactions per second. Ethereum is using a few new methods to accomplish this scale, while still prioritizing security. Another big Ethereum update, related to energy consumption, is moving from proof-of-work consensus (like Bitcoin uses) to proof-of-stake consensus. In proof-of-work, a ton of energy is consumed in the form of computing power, but it's also this "work" that helps keep miners honest. In proof-of-stake, it's the stipulated "stake" that keeps the miners honest. If a miner approves a dishonest transaction, then their stake—usually an expensive amount of Ethereum's currency called "Ether"—is slashed. This method of consensus requires much less energy consumption than the Bitcoin network because miners do less "work" in order to validate the next block (Land, 2021).

In summary, Vitalik Buterin has developed the crucial next evolution of cryptocurrency with Ethereum. The vibrant Ethereum community of open-source developers is responsible for its continued success, which is a remarkable feat for a decentralized network. It is now possible to have almost anything on the internet be created as a blockchain-based application. There are already over three thousand decentralized applications powered by Ethereum in various categories like gambling and online marketplaces. The future is ripe with potential because of Vitalik's vision for blockchain technology.

ETHAN TURER AND CHALLENGE COIN

If Bitcoin is the first evolution of cryptocurrency, and Ethereum is the second, then Challenge Coin will be the third.

In 2014, when I was still a high school student, I was very interested in safety and emergency preparedness. I got involved in the Community Emergency Response Team (CERT) for community first responders and even started the Safety Club. I thought it would be worthwhile for other teenagers in the San Fernando Valley to learn lifesaving skills like using a fire extinguisher and performing CPR. I organized the first ever Teen CERT class for the San Fernando

Valley. After eight weeks of three-hour long class instruction from Fire Captain Christopher Cooper, a group of around thirty teenagers graduated as recognized community emergency responders.

The ceremony included Los Angeles Mayor Eric Garcetti staff and Councilmember Mitchell Englander, who awarded each graduate for their commitment to serving the community. When it was my turn, I was honored to also receive a Challenge Coin from the councilman. He explained, "In the First World War, many wealthy Americans from Ivy League schools joined the squadrons in Europe. A lieutenant from Yale decided to give bronze challenge coins to his unit, and one young pilot placed the coin in a pouch around his neck. In short order, he was shot down by the Germans."

Councilmember Englander continued, "That pilot was then stripped of his belongings except for his pouch [and coin]. During a daring escape, he reached French lines but wary of saboteurs, the French chose to execute him. With little time, the pilot revealed his coin—and loyalties—and instead of a firing squad, received a good bottle of Bordeaux." This coin represents providing a great service to your community, and you're supposed to carry it with you as a challenge to go above and beyond, and to be a better person (Lammle, 2012).

Challenge Coin is very meaningful to me, but it is also the perfect name to challenge others to be the best they can be. We all experience personal challenges in our lives, and it takes strength to overcome them. We are also faced with some of the biggest challenges of our generation, including climate change, a global pandemic, and wealth inequality.

I believe everyone has the power to change the world for the better. Cryptocurrency is the digital currency for the people, by the people, and it empowers each individual to control their money.

The next breakthrough in digital currency is also an evolution in how people think about money and their worth. Bitcoin made it possible for currency to operate independent of governments and banks. Ethereum made it possible for blockchain to be more than just currency and transactions. Challenge Coin will be a cryptocurrency that empowers people by capturing the value of their worth. Every person will have their own Challenge Coin, which is tied to their value.

Currently people associate their worth with their occupation. You have a salary and title, and that's how most people determine their worth. If you get rich enough, then you accumulate assets like a house, car, stocks, and bonds. The total value of your tangible or physical assets, minus any outstanding debt, is your net worth. But people are more than the assets they accumulate over time. We also build relationships, good will, personal brands, internet followings, and many more intangible assets.

The internet has created unimaginable opportunity and value for people, but most of that value is collected by central entities like banks and corporations. Today everyone is failing at capturing their total worth, tangible and intangible assets, but cryptocurrency can fix that. Challenge Coin will be the cryptocurrency that solves this problem and so many more.

CHAPTER 2

Money, Fiat Currency, and Cryptocurrency

––––

THE FALL OF THE ROMAN EMPIRE

Famous philosopher, George Santayana,
in his work *The Life of Reason* said,
"Those who cannot remember the past
are condemned to repeat it."

In order not to repeat the collapse of currencies, we must look to our past. The fall of the Roman Empire is a story that may sound similar to our current circumstances. Pay close attention to how the Romans debased their currency, gold, and the impact it had on their society.

Julius Caesar created the aureus coin, which contained around eight grams of gold. This coin was widely accepted across Europe and the Mediterranean for seventy-five years until Emperor Nero started the practice of coin clipping. This meant that a small piece of those gold coins would be broken off so the government could melt the clips down and make more gold coins. This process led to price inflation because of the increase of supply of currency that normally drives up the price of goods (Ammous, 2018).

While this was happening, the Roman Empire kept expanding through war. This was an expensive proposition, so the aureus coin, which started at eight grams, was debased with other metals. This meant that its gold value was reduced over time and replaced with cheaper metals, like silver and bronze. Eventually, the real value of the coin lowered to a point where the economy suffered (Maloney, 2018).

Rome went through this currency debasement cycle many times to pay for war and expansion. Finally, in 301 AD, Emperor Diocletian had to deal with the worsening inflation problem of the Roman Empire. He increased deficit spending with jobs programs for the homeless and other public works programs. This only made the problem worse until the first ever incident of hyperinflation occurred (Maloney, 2015).

In the book *A Guide to Investing in Gold and Silver*, Mike Maloney explains, "In Diocletian's Edict of Prices a pound of gold was worth 50,000 denari in the year AD 301, but by mid-century was worth 2.12 billion denari. That means the price of gold rose 42,400 times in fifty or so years. This resulted in all currency-based trade coming to a virtual standstill, and the economic system reverted to a barter system."

Diocletian imposed his "Edict of Prices," which was a set of rules for price controls of goods, services, and wages. By trying to control the prices of goods, he was just putting a Band-Aid on a fatal wound. After that, the downfall of the Roman Empire was inevitable. Rioting, corruption, lawlessness, and mania spread throughout the empire like a plague (Lips, 2002).

Mike Maloney warns, "This pattern of failed price controls is something we see throughout history and across the globe.... It's worth noting that when wage and price controls are implemented, the government always tries to deflect attention away from the problems that it has created."

The United States has some eerie parallels to the fall of the Roman Empire. In order to understand how similar these two stories are, let's fast forward to 1971.

An important event in American history that's often overlooked, is when the US dollar changed from being backed by gold to being backed by nothing but trust in the government. With inflation rising and a fear of a gold run, President Nixon addressed the nation, saying, "The time has come for a new economic policy for the United States. Its targets are unemployment, inflation, and international speculation. And this is how we are going to attack those targets."

President Nixon continued, "The strength of a nation's currency is based on the strength of that nation's economy—and the American economy is by far the strongest in the world. Accordingly, I have directed the Secretary of the Treasury to take the action necessary to defend the dollar against the speculators. I have directed Secretary Connally to suspend temporarily the convertibility of the dollar into gold or other reserve assets, except in amounts and conditions determined to be in the interest of monetary stability and in the best interests of the United States."

Just like how the Roman Empire began the process of debasing their currency from real gold to remnants of it, the US dollar was debased from being tethered to gold to there being no intrinsic value at all. From that point, US currency was no longer money, but fiat currency. Fiat, for all intents and purposes, stands for fake. It's as if Richard Nixon said from that day on, we would use Monopoly money as our primary currency. Except this fake currency is backed by the US government through its "strength in the nation's economy."

Only two years after President Nixon made that infamous monetary policy change, inflation began to rise just like it did in the Roman Empire. Nixon stated, "Every American family is confronted with a real and pressing problem of higher prices. And I have decided that the time has come to take strong and effective action to deal with that problem. Effective immediately, therefore, I am ordering a freeze on prices. This freeze will hold prices at levels no higher than those charged during the first eight days of June. It will cover all prices paid by consumers."

Since that time, the price of goods has increased significantly. Inflationtool.com states, "The inflation rate in the United States between 1971 and today has been 546.85 percent, which translates into a total increase of $546.85. This means that 100 dollars in 1971 are equivalent to 646.85 dollars in 2020.

In other words, the purchasing power of $100 in 1971 equals $646.85 today. The average annual inflation rate has been 3.8 percent."

Let's put that into context. Imagine you are back in 1971 and you go to the store with $100. You would be able to buy a lot with that money because the price of goods was lower. If you were at the store today, you would need around $650 to buy the same items you would be able to buy with $100 back in 1971. That's inflation in a nutshell.

Today, the US dollar is "clipped," like the aureus coin was, in a few ways as well. The value of the dollar has decreased over time due to inflation. The price of consumer goods has increased, but product shrinkage is also clipping away at the real value of the consumer's dollar. For example, food inflation is a clever way that companies charge more for less, essentially clipping away at the real value of the dollar. Have you noticed that ice cream, cereal, and candy bars aren't as big as they used to be? That's food inflation (Dickler, 2008).

The signs of impending doom are told throughout history, and if we do not take action to mitigate this collapse, then we're likely going to see a fate similar to the one the Roman Empire faced. Gold has outlasted all other currencies for thousands of years. In the next section, we will explore what makes gold a great currency and how Bitcoin may take that title.

MONEY VS. CURRENCY

In the same way that the Roman Empire used gold as its primary currency, there have been many goods and commodities that have been used as currency, including seashells and rare rocks. Almost anything can be a currency if it has the following properties: medium of exchange, unit of account, portable, durable, divisible, and fungible (Maloney, 2013).

Money has the same properties of currency with the additional quality of being a *store of value* for a long period of time. Notice that money is different from currency in that money will maintain its value over time. Gold is a perfect example of money because it still remains valuable after thousands of years (Team, 2018).

Let's dive into what the properties of money are and why they matter. *The Bitcoin Standard* explains that there used to be direct exchange between two people. They would exchange goods and services, similar to bartering, or any other way of exchanging goods directly. Through direct exchange, you could trade one chicken for two fish, for instance.

That's a completely legitimate way to trade goods. The problem is that once you expand that trade outside of the small community, things become more complicated. There needs to be a more trusted *medium of exchange,* and so the medium is like the intermediary between goods—the good that everyone agrees is primarily used as the exchange for other goods is currency.

A wide acceptance of a medium of exchange means that the prices of goods can be expressed by it or as a *unit of account.*

Think of it like a common denominator for communicating value. For example, a certain weight of gold is worth this chicken, but then this lesser weight of gold is worth this fish. So instead of trading a portion of a chicken for a whole fish you could trade gold as the intermediary. This makes it a lot easier to calculate prices of goods if everyone is using the same metrics for measuring value.

Portable is the property that enables money to move across distances. Cattle were once used as currency, but they were not easily portable, so they were only used for larger purchases. *Durable* means that the currency will last a long time. Apples are not durable because they quickly decay and lose their intrinsic value: your ability to eat them.

Divisible is the property of scale. Gold can be used in varying weights and the US dollar comes in different amounts ($100, $50, $20, etc.). Lastly, *fungible* means that the currency is interchangeable. The dollar in one person's wallet has the exact same value as the dollar in someone else's wallet.

In 1636, Europeans adopted seashells as legal tender for a medium of exchange. It only took twenty-five years for seashells to lose their status as legal tender, or cash, and have no monetary role. What happened? Advanced boats were able to harvest large quantities of seashells to the point where they lost all value. The societies that used seashells as a medium of exchange essentially transferred their wealth to the seashell producers. This pattern of goods being used as currency, then being devalued through mass production and new supply of that good occurs many times throughout history.

Slavery can actually be tied to this destructive wealth transfer process as well. In the sixteenth century, Europeans visited West Africa where small glass beads were the primary form of currency. The Europeans saw an opportunity for arbitrage of the cheap-to-produce glass beads in exchange for most of the resources of the Africans. The glass beads became known as "slave beads" for their role in impoverishing the Africans.

The Roman Empire and colonial Europe both teach us an important lesson: the medium of exchange we decide to accept as a society can lead to our downfall if we're not careful. Let's explore the US dollar and whether it meets all the necessary properties of money and/or currency.

Since 1971, the US Dollar (USD) has been fiat currency. It holds no intrinsic value because you can no longer exchange it for gold. Our trust in the promise that the US government and Federal Reserve will maintain the value of the dollar is what gives the dollar value. The whole world uses the US dollar as the reserve, or default, currency so there is a lot at stake.

The USD is a medium of exchange because you can use it to buy other goods. It's a unit of account since we all set prices of goods in terms of USD. It's portable because it's not heavy and can fit in your wallet. It's relatively durable and doesn't break too easily. The USD is divisible because you can use different denominations (quarters, dimes, nickels, pennies). Lastly, it's fungible, meaning that two people with different $20 bills can buy the same good. We can conclude that the USD is a currency.

The million-dollar question: Is the US dollar a good store of value? Personally, I don't think it is, however, you might get a different answer depending on who you talk to. Like I demonstrated earlier, inflation since the seventies has already devalued the currency, meaning it has struggled to hold its value for the past fifty years. Compared to gold, which is money, fiat currencies have not been able to store value for long periods of time. If you look at past events to decide, then you might come to the same conclusion that the USD is currency and not money.

So now we've learned that your true wealth is your time and your freedom. Money is a trading tool that stores the economic energy that is your time and freedom whereas currencies leak them away. Gold and silver are the ultimate money simply because of their properties. Fiat currencies are based solely on confidence and always return to their intrinsic value of zero. Governments don't like gold because it imposes restraint. Rising prices are a symptom of an expanding currency supply and gold and silver always account for an expanding currency supply (Maloney, 2013).

BITCOIN: CURRENCY OR MONEY?

A little after a year since the first Bitcoin transaction was recorded in 2009, its value in USD was a fraction of a cent, basically zero. In May 2010, programmer Laszlo Hanyecz became the first person to use Bitcoin (BTC) as a medium of exchange. He bought two large Papa John's pizzas for ten thousand Bitcoins. He paid someone in Europe to order

Hanyecz those pizzas for delivery to his home in Jacksonville, Florida (Merchant, 2013).

Those 10,000 BTC were worth around $40 USD. At the end of 2020, Bitcoin reached a peak of over $28,000. That makes this pizza purchase one of the most expensive in history at $280 million and counting. This story is famous throughout Bitcoin folklore and is commemorated as Bitcoin Pizza Day, which is celebrated on May 22 (Moore, 2020).

Hanyecz holds no regrets from making that costly pizza purchase. Back then, he was a believer in the use of Bitcoin as real money, and without early adopters like him, Bitcoin may never have become the store of value people invest in today. It's a catch-22 of sorts, and Hanyecz opted for a future where Bitcoin could be a medium of exchange, not just a digital asset from which to make money.

The price fluctuations of Bitcoin in the last decade have shown that Bitcoin is not a good medium of exchange. Since the value keeps changing, it's not a great store of value either, so right now it doesn't look like it will be a good replacement as a global currency. This property of Bitcoin can change in the long run because of how Satoshi Nakamoto programmed the supply of Bitcoin to change.

For every two hundred ten thousand new blocks that are created, or on average every four years, a halving takes place to control inflation. The reward for mining Bitcoin halves in order to adjust with the ever-increasing price of Bitcoin. Eventually, the total Bitcoin that can ever be mined, which is twenty-one million, will be reached. We have already mined over eighteen million Bitcoin, so the supply of Bitcoin will become more and more scarce over time (Hayes, 2021).

This process of halving gives Bitcoin a natural deflationary property, which is unique compared to gold and fiat currencies. Bitcoin is extremely divisible because you can trade it in fractions, and it's programmed to halve its reward until the last Bitcoin block is mined, unlike gold—which is constantly being mined—and the USD, which has printed trillions of new units of currency into existence in the last decade (Coppola, 2020).

Cryptocurrencies' volatility in price is the crux keeping it from being adopted as a currency. It's not the best alternative to the US dollar yet. When it becomes a better alternative, that's when you'll see adoption happen more. Generally, people don't want to spend millions of dollars on pizza. Bitcoin is not usable yet for everyday purposes like going to buy groceries.

Let's quickly see if Bitcoin holds the other properties of currency. We have already discussed that it's divisible. It's durable in that it cannot be destroyed or manipulated digitally by a third party. It's portable across space through the internet and can record transactions globally. It is fungible, as a Bitcoin for one person has the same buying power as another person's Bitcoin. Technically, it can be a unit of account, but with price fluctuations, it's not the best currency for that, either.

Bitcoin isn't the only game in town, though. Stablecoins are another Bitcoin alternative. These are cryptocurrencies specifically designed to have a stable price, and they avoid the pitfalls of Bitcoin's price volatility. Tether is an example of a stablecoin that connected its price to the US dollar. It is pegged against the USD and maintains a one-to-one ratio with it in terms of value ("Tether," 2014).

Stablecoins offer a glimpse of how cryptocurrencies may become the next world reserve currency. Bitcoin is the technological foundation that made possible an alternative to fiat currency in the digital world. When looking to the future, it's important to remember the patterns of the past. Bitcoin may not be the next world reserve currency, but cryptocurrencies are already rising to the challenge.

Anthony Lewis, the author of *The Basics of Bitcoins and Blockchains* says:

> *Bitcoin may be suffering growing pains in its infancy, but this doesn't mean we should write it off and that the story must end here.... It seems that people try to fit Bitcoin into an existing bucket, and when it exhibits some properties that do not match others in that bucket, it is declared a failure. Maybe the answer is to not try to fit it into any existing bucket, but to design or define a new bucket, and judge Bitcoin and other cryptoassets on their own merits.*

CHAPTER 3

Bubbles: Build, Burst, Repeat

THE CALIFORNIA GOLD RUSH

Bubbles have existed throughout time. People find an opportunity and get excited about it. They are so excited that they go to their friends and get them excited about it. This process continues until the opportunity is in such high demand that it far exceeds its actual value. That's when the bubble bursts. People start panic selling because all their friends are selling. This cycle existed in the past, exists now, and will likely exist far into the future.

The California Gold Rush was a bubble that got people excited about the prospect of prospecting gold. Throughout the world, tales of riches were told about people who stepped off the boat and almost immediately found large nuggets of gold. These tales were so captivating that about three hundred thousand people made the treacherous trip across oceans to settle down in California.

Unfortunately, for those who survived the trip, their lives were not easy, nor were they immediately rich. Some gold miners spent their entire lives and all their money sifting through dirt and never found any gold. The people who did find gold became rich, and those were the stories that made it across oceans—the successes, not the failures.

In an interview with J. R. Willet, inventor of the initial coin offering (ICO), he retells a story from his father:

> *During the Gold Rush, it wasn't the gold miners that made the money. It was Levi Strauss and the various people that were selling stuff to the gold miners [that did]. The guys that had the places that sold the pickaxes, the shovels, the stores, and various other unsavory businesses that sprung up all around the Gold Rush. They were the people that made the real money.*

Today, California is a prosperous economy because of the mass migration from the Gold Rush, but if people knew the truth about who was actually getting rich, and the many people that never did, then maybe the Gold Rush wouldn't have been such a rush at all.

I'm not arguing that bubbles are bad or good. They just are. It's a natural part of the human experience because it taps into our greediness, our fear of missing out, and our dreams of the future. Let's explore one of the first bubbles of the internet era, the Dot-com Bubble.

DOT-COM BUBBLE

The internet, or Dot-com, bubble of the early 2000s was an exciting time for entrepreneurs. Everyone wanted to be a part of this new frontier. Domain names became a popular way to own parts of the internet, like pets.com or toys.com. Most of the companies that formed during this time failed once the internet bubble burst. Only a few made it big, like Amazon and Google, because they had a business model that wasn't purely built on hype.

The *Los Angeles Times* summarized the huge losses from the Dot-com bubble: "The late-1990s bubble that began to implode in 2000, wiping out within two years $5 trillion in paper wealth on Nasdaq, the stock market on which the shares of many tech companies are traded. The market value of Nasdaq companies peaked at $6.7 trillion in March 2000 and bottomed out at $1.6 trillion in October 2002" (Gaither and Chmielewski, 2006).

The mentality from investors at the time was to buy nearly anything associated with the internet, regardless of valuation. Investors didn't care about internet companies not making a profit or taking huge losses. The price-to-earnings ratio (P/E) is a metric for investors to figure out if a stock's price is overvalued or undervalued. According to *Investopedia*, "The average P/E for the S&P 500 has historically ranged from 13 to 15" (Murphy, 2021). At the time of the Dot-com bubble, investors were willing to pay over one hundred times their expected earnings (Kleinbard, 2000).

The internet became the international tool it is today because of that bubble. Bubbles are almost like a milestone for a growing industry. People want to be a part of the excitement even if they lack the understanding of the underlying technology. Even today, most people probably don't understand how the internet works. I don't know how to code the ones and zeros that made it possible to write the text on my computer. It's okay to not know everything, but to only invest because others are also investing is a recipe for disaster when it comes to bubbles.

HOUSING BUBBLE

In 2008, not long after the internet bubble, the housing market collapsed, which led to the Great Recession in the United States. The madness of crowds is a common description of bubbles because it takes the irrational behavior of many people for bubbles to inflate and then burst. The housing bubble was no exception.

The American Dream is often connected to homeownership as a path to success and opportunity. How does homeownership become a bubble? It started with lenders, like Fannie Mae, relaxing lending standards so that people with bad credit or who could not afford to pay back a mortgage qualified for loans. The demand for homes skyrocketed, which led to a price increase in those homes. The cycle repeated until housing prices reached a tipping point in 2006 and 2007 (Lusk, 2019).

That's only half the story, though. The housing bubble led to a Great Recession because of the greedy and irrational behavior of Wall Street based on the housing market. Subprime mortgage-backed securities were the speculative instruments that took down Bear Stearns, an investment bank, and almost the entire US economy as well. When housing mania reached its tipping point, the greater fools—the ones left holding the bag—were the financial institutions and banks that were over-leveraged on these bad speculative investments.

On September 29, 2008, the stock market experienced one of its worst days in history. The Dow Jones Industrial Average had the largest single-day loss, falling 777.68 points. Other investment banks like Lehman Brothers went bankrupt, so the US government stepped in to try to stop the dominoes from falling even further. The bailout of almost a trillion dollars saved the auto, airline, and financial industries who were too big to fail (Nankin and Schmidt, 2009).

Even giant institutions like investment banks are susceptible to bubbles. The key pattern to look out for is speculative behavior detached from the true value of the asset. If you don't know what the true value of something is, then look at its historical prices to compare them. The housing bubble was the biggest bubble in modern history until the 2017 cryptocurrency bubble.

CRYPTOCURRENCY BUBBLE

Bitcoin was created in 2009 and was only worth pennies at that time. By 2017, it had reached a broader appeal and captivated the imagination of many people. It reached an all-time high of nearly $20,000 and then subsequently crashed to around $3,000 (Coindesk, 2021). According to Burton Malkiel, author of *Random Walk Down Wall Street*, the Bitcoin bubble was one of the biggest of all time; bigger than both the Dot-com bubble and housing bubble.

The reason Bitcoin's price dropped so spectacularly is that people were investing emotionally based on hype and per- ceived value from the sentiment of crowds. If everyone that bought Bitcoin in 2017 did their due diligence and saw the cryptocurrency's potential for the long term, then I don't think they would have panic sold when the price started to fall. I believe an informed investor is less likely to be affected by the madness of crowds.

By 2021, Bitcoin reached over $50,000, which was more than double the all-time high of the 2017 bubble. So, are we in another bubble? What makes something a bubble? Are these bubbles going to keep happening?

I invested in Bitcoin in 2018 as the price was falling because I thought I could buy the dip. Well after I bought Bitcoin, the price continued to fall but instead of selling, I bought more. I thought Bitcoin was the currency of the future and planned to hold that investment for a few years at least.

Fast forward to 2020, the price of Bitcoin had more than recovered and my investment was finally profitable. When the price of Bitcoin passed $20,000 for the first time, I assumed that people would start selling so I decided to sell my holdings at around $25,000. Only a couple months later, Bitcoin had a new all-time high of nearly $60,000, spurred by institutional investors, like MicroStrategy.

The price of Bitcoin crashed again to around $30,000, or half of its all-time high. These price fluctuations are indicative of a bubble in the unregulated and manipulated internet era. The value of Bitcoin is still unknown, so all investors can do is speculate on its future worth. Someday, Bitcoin may reach mass adoption all around the world, which would justify even higher prices for a scarce asset. Today, Bitcoin is still in its early stages, so prices are based on the sentiment of crowds and perceived value.

Even I, author of this book, did not follow my own advice. Let my story of trying to time the market be forever ingrained in your memory. Sure, I made some money, but my logic was irrational. I tried to predict the future by remembering the past. In the end, I was no better than the millions of speculators before me.

Technology will ultimately greatly improve the intentional payments system, and there will always be advantages to holding an asset that is anonymous and transportable without a physical trace. Yet, the lessons of history are immutable. Speculative bubbles will persist, and they ultimately lead most of their participants to financial ruin. Even real technological revolutions do not guarantee benefits for investors (Malkiel, 2020).

THE NEXT BIG BUBBLE

There is a common view amongst cryptocurrency investors about what the next big bubble will be and how it will burst. No one can predict the future and the series of events that lead to a bubble, but I will do my best to convey this shared understanding.

Most people who believe in the future of cryptocurrencies are highly skeptical of central authorities like governments and banks. Thus, it's no wonder that cryptocurrency believers think that the next big bubble will be caused by those very institutions.

Here's a bold statement: The US dollar is a house of cards.

This means that the USD is a fiat currency, which has no intrinsic value, and no foundation to its worth. If tomorrow everyone realized that our collective delusion was keeping the value of USD afloat, then it could crash almost immediately. That sounds like a very scary situation and one that is highly unlikely, but I think it's worth exploring because the reality might not be that far off from this nightmarish theory.

Remember how the financial world almost collapsed in 2008 because of the housing crisis? What if I told you that was just a precursor to what is coming next?

The next big bubble will be a societal reckoning, the scale of which we have never seen before. This bubble is an intersection of things that are not working in society like the USD, Federal Reserve, Wall Street, and wealth inequality.

Lance Roberts, author of *Real Investment Advice PRO*, explains the serious ramifications of the "everything bubble": "The US economy is literally on perpetual life support. Recent events show too clearly that unless fiscal and monetary stimulus continues, the economy will fail and, by extension, the stock market." The Federal Reserve has lowered interest rates to provide liquidity to the market. This artificially inflates the economy along with quantitative easing, which pumps trillions of dollars into it.

Without these drastic measures from the Federal Reserve, Lance Roberts argues, that the everything bubble will burst. He warns, "What the average person fails to understand is that the next 'financial crisis' will not just be a stock market crash, a housing bust, or a collapse in bond prices. It could be the simultaneous implosion of all three" (Roberts, 2021).

In the scenario where a bubble this massive bursts, the US government would likely get involved again like it did in the 2008 housing bubble. Bailing out all the industries impacted by the everything bubble would take trillions and trillions of dollars. Before the bailout in 2008, there was around $900 billion in assets held by the Federal Reserve. After a decade of bailouts and quantitative easing, the balance sheet of the Fed is over $8 trillion ("Federal Reserve Board - Recent Balance Sheet Trends", 2021).

The dramatic increase in fiat currency printed out of thin air in the last decade is cause for concern, and cryptocurrency investors are taking notice. The fear is that if the behavior continues, then the USD will experience hyperinflation similar to the one that occurred in Zimbabwe. The abundance of the Zimbabwean currency led to inflation where their currency had less purchasing power. In response to the inflation, the government printed even more currency, with higher denominations.

That is how the $100 trillion Zimbabwean note came into existence. Eventually, the dollar became worthless as a medium of exchange. There was more utility in burning the dollars for a fire than using them to buy goods and services. In 2015, the government decided to abandon its currency entirely, instead using the US dollar and other local currencies (Whitbourne and Guzman, 2021).

The US dollar is essentially the same as the Zimbabwean currency in that it is fiat. There is nothing stopping the USD from experiencing the same fate as all the other fiat currencies before it. Bitcoin has a limited supply, which makes it deflationary as the value continues to increase over time. Cryptocurrency investors believe that Bitcoin is a hedge against the US dollar because it's a digital currency that's independent from the control of central authorities like the Federal Reserve.

Bubbles have existed and will continue to exist for years to come. The bubbles of the modern era are more interconnected because of the internet and have gotten bigger than ever. The next bubble or the everything bubble may mean the collapse of industries and institutions like we have never seen before—that's if the beliefs of cryptocurrency investors are true. Just like anyone trying to predict the future, only time will tell.

CHAPTER 4

Debt: Trap or Tool?

———

To understand the significance of cryptocurrency, it's worth exploring the beginnings of debt as a tool and how it has transformed over time.

What is debt? In theory, it is a tool that allows people to borrow money they don't have, to make a purchase now (usually of a house, car, higher education, or other high-cost items) and pay back their balances in the future. This tool is a powerful way for people to increase their quality of life, assuming that they will be able to pay back their loans when they are due. In practice, it is a trap for lenders and big companies to take advantage of consumers and squeeze them out of any asset they have been able to save up.

If you can't afford to pay the loan, then you risk losing your home, car, or any collateral you put down when you agreed to go into debt. Another, sometimes worse, debt trap is where interest rates go up every time you miss a payment or can't pay the full amount due. So, the debt spirals out of control because you are only paying the interest on the loan and never paying off the principal or original amount borrowed.

This is how big credit card companies make so much money by offering individuals the option to pay the minimum of their balance every month. Meanwhile the interest rates and principal of the total amount due can increase exponentially such that you may never make enough money in the future to pay it off.

Right now is an important time for us to take a step back and analyze whether certain human institutions, like debt, are working the way they were intended. Or, has debt become another failed collective illusion that actually traps a vast majority of people into a state of perpetual anxiety about their next bill? Most Americans are living paycheck to paycheck with little to no savings, dreading the next emergency that puts them further into debt (Fay, 2019).

In this chapter we'll explore the history of debt, its efficacy, how it has impacted our lives, and a future where debt doesn't have to be the scary trap that it has become.

HISTORY OF DEBT

"The moment one casts matters on a broad historical scale, though, the first thing one learns is that there's nothing new about virtual money. Actually, this was the original form of money. Credit system, tabs, even expense accounts, all existed long before cash. These things are as old as civilization itself" (Graeber, 2021).

The origin of debt is quite interesting when you think about how debt is currently used today. David Graeber is a famous anthropologist, professor, and author. His book, *Debt: The*

First 5,000 Years, talks about a common misconception that debt started as a barter system. Most students learn about bartering in a historical context as the foundation of how our ancestors exchanged goods and services thousands of years ago. However, Graeber explains that there is no anthropological evidence that that system actually existed.

Barter is easier to explain, so it continues to be taught in our educational institutions: "Once upon a time, there was barter. It was difficult. So, people invented money. Then came the development of banking and credit" (Graeber, 2021). In reality, what happened is that debt was actually a credit system among neighbors in a community with members that were indebted to one another. These community members would borrow from each other with the expectation of receiving something of similar value in return. There was no money exchanged but instead a system of trust and credit. Since they're keeping track of what's owed to them, at the end of a year, there would be a communal reckoning where all debts were paid, and the credit system would start again at zero (Strauss, 2016).

We started with virtual money and accounting, where members of a community trusted each other to pay back their debts. What is a debt then, historically speaking? In essence, it's an obligation to another party. These obligations were not transferable, however, because they lacked a medium of exchange. That's where money and currency came in. Graeber says, "Not only is it money that makes debt possible: money and debt appear on the scene at exactly the same time. Some of the very first written documents that have come down to us are Mesopotamian tablets recording credits and debits, rations issued by temples, money owed for rent of temple lands, the value of each precisely specified in grain and silver" (Graeber, 2021).

Graeber continues, "Some of the earliest works of moral philosophy, in turn, are reflections on what it means to imagine morality as debt—that is, in terms of money. A history of debt, then, is thus necessarily a history of money and the easiest way to understand the role that debt has played in human society is simply to follow the forms that money has taken, and the way money has been used, across the centuries" (Graeber, 2021). The evolution of debt goes hand in hand with money. Money was actually invented to pay soldiers. Governments needed a way to employ soldiers that was more effective than credit. Also, soldiers were putting their lives on the line, so they could not wait a year to be paid back. The state created currency and then began accepting taxes with this new currency. Then, you had a state-run currency that was a medium of exchange for all members of its kingdom. This is also how the first markets were created as a side effect of military operations.

Then, as giant governments—such as the Roman Empire—began to fail, churches started to fill the void that was left behind. During the Middle Ages, churches returned to power and brought back the older systems of credit. Goods were still valued using the old currencies as a unit of account, but there was no physical currency exchanging hands. Fast forward to the 1400s, when gold and silver starts coming back from the Americas. Slavery and government empires start to dominate society, which leads to globalization, and currencies once again become the main form of debt tracking.

And this is how we've structured our current system of debt (Graeber, 2021).

The power players have changed, but the underlying system is the same. Following World War II, the United States of America emerged as the main power, and the US dollar became the reserve currency for the world. This all happened at Bretton Woods, New Hampshire in 1944, where forty-four nations convened to determine the world's new financial system. The World Bank and International Monetary Fund (IMF) also came into existence at this historic conference (Rosalsky, 2019).

In the 1970s, the US currency changed from a gold-backed currency to fiat. This means that we have yet again moved to virtual money, except instead of trusting each other within a small community, we trust the US government to maintain the world's currency. Then, in 2008, with the creation of a decentralized digital currency called Bitcoin, we had the ability to trust each other again, except this time through the internet, which encompasses the world.

DEBT: PRESENT DAY
The following is a fictional story based on research of many real-life experiences in the United States:

Sam woke up like it was any normal day. He made breakfast with his wife of three years, Lily. They recently bought a home together and were expecting a baby in a few months. If it was a girl, they'd name her Beth, and if it was a boy, they'd name him Tom. Sam worked at a reputable insurance company and Lily was working on finishing her degree in nursing. They met at UCLA in biology class while they were in a study group together. Their story was like many of their peers in that they found love and decided to start a family after college. The difference was that in an instant, it all came crashing down.

While Sam was almost done with work, processing medical insurance claims, Lily was out grocery shopping. It was peak shopping time, with many people rushing to get their food and make dinner for their families. As Lily was making a left hand turn out of the shopping center, another driver rushed through a red light, and in that instant, everything changed. Sam got the call from the hospital that his wife had been in a serious collision and that he needed to come quick. His heart fell to the floor as he imagined the worst-case scenario. Unfortunately for Sam, it was far worse than he could have imagined.

After Sam frantically arrived at the local hospital, he was greeted by staff who tried to calm him down and explain the situation. Lily was not doing well. She had multiple broken bones, internal bleeding, head trauma, and it was possible that she would never walk again. Even worse is that their baby had died. This news hit Sam like a dump truck crashing into a brick wall. He was hysterical and barely knew what to do as his life felt like it was falling apart all around him. The bad news was far from over as other realities started to rush to the surface: "Were all of these treatments being covered by my insurance? Do I have enough saved up to pay for these expenses? What happens if Lily doesn't make it? Can I afford to pay for funeral costs?"

After a month of recovery and many invasive surgeries, Lily was finally in stable condition. Even as she was recovering physically, the reality of the financial trouble the couple was in became apparent. Bills began to pile up, and Sam and Lily soon realized how insurmountable the medical debt would be. Even with Sam's background in insurance, there were costs that were not covered, including the out-of-network surgeons. The expenses that were covered by insurance after the hefty $5,000 deductible paled in comparison to the many medical bills that they would face in the years to come.

In addition, the car was totaled, and the car insurance company put the fault on Lily, since she was making a left turn, and there were no witnesses that corroborated that the other driver was speeding through a red light. Legal bills and fees started coming in as the driver of the other vehicle filed suit against them for their own medical bills. All in all, in an instant, Lily and Sam went from being excited about the future and starting a family to being buried in medical, legal, and other debt totaling over $200,000.

This story is not unique. The reality is that health care costs are the number one cause of bankruptcy in the United States. And over one hundred thirty-seven million Americans have experienced financial hardship because of medical costs (Konish, 2019). If the problem was only medical bills, then we'd pass some form of "Medicare for All" legislation so that a vast majority of Americans could sleep a little easier knowing that they aren't going to have to go into medical debt. However, the debt problem far surpasses just medical bills, unfortunately.

Let's go back to Sam and Lily as an example. What if Sam lost his job after Lily's accident? What if he lost his medical coverage? In America, if you don't have a job, then you're basically screwed unless you make so little that you can get covered by a public option like Medicaid. Remember the house Sam was working toward owning? Well, without a job, how is Sam going to pay the mortgage payments? Getting evicted from your own home is not an experience anyone should have to go through, and yet around four million people on average get evicted every year in America (Benfer et al., 2020).

So far, we've talked about medical debt and housing debt, but many other forms of debt exist, plaguing almost every American. The New York Federal Reserve reports on non-housing debt—student loans, credit cards, auto loans, and other consumer debts—which are forms of debt that do not include housing and mortgage debt. Americans are up to their eyeballs in debt from car payments to credit card debt and student loan debt. 2020 marked the highest debt levels on record, totaling over $4 trillion in non-housing debt for Americans.

Every year, a new record is set for the number of indebted Americans, and every year, we pretend like this amount of debt is sustainable for people in the long term. We cannot keep pretending that this human institution is working for most people when few opportunities exist to dig yourself out of a systematic hole that was designed to keep you trapped inside it.

Debt traps have become a vehicle for modern day slavery, as Derek Sall from "Life and My Finances" explains:

Today, 80 percent of [Americans] offer ourselves to modern day slavery. No, we don't need to literally put ourselves to work on our master's property, but every time we buy something on payments, we tell that manufacturer/builder/business owner that we'll give them a portion of our future earnings—that's money that we don't even have yet! We're selling our tomorrows for the trinkets and shiny objects of today. It's causing us to save less, to invest less, and we then need to work later in life because of it. Consumerism is quite literally a voluntary slavery program, but unfortunately, very few of us realize it until it's too late.

THE FUTURE OF DEBT

Now imagine a world where the debt trap was obsolete and replaced with an investment structure similar to the credit systems back in the day. It's hard to do, isn't it? This kind of human institution already exists in different forms. The stock market is a system wherein companies can release their stock to the public, which allows anyone in that market to invest and own shares of that company. When an investor owns shares in the company, there is no debt relationship since the value of the investment comes from the appreciation of the asset over time.

Compared to a bond where you are basically paying back a loan at an agreed-upon time or maturity date, stocks are highly volatile, but the risk can be rewarded as the value of the stock goes up. Stocks and bonds are human institutions that currently exist primarily for businesses and big organizations to benefit from, however. An individual can invest in both stocks and bonds, but according to a Gallup Poll, 45 percent of Americans do not participate in the stock market at all.

What would a human institution look like that allowed people to invest in each other? Let's revisit Sam and Lily, who have gone through many hardships in a relatively short amount of time. In our current system, they have a few options, and most aren't very favorable. First, they can declare bankruptcy, since the amount of bills has reached a point where they will never get out from the hole they are in. Declaring bankruptcy would allow them to settle some of their debts—but not all of them. Student loan debt and government taxes are still owed after you declare bankruptcy. And it negatively impacts your credit score, so if you ever need a loan in the future, debtors will know that you went bankrupt in the past.

It can, however, stop banks from foreclosing your home, which is a major benefit of the process. This option is a last resort for most people for all the reasons listed above. What else can Sam and Lily do? Many people, when in a serious financial situation like the one Sam and Lily went through, reach out to friends and family for help with paying back their debt. Let's say, for this example, that no one has that kind of money to help. Then, there's a new phenomenon where people with unexpected life circumstances start an online crowdfunding campaign to appeal to the masses.

This option is relatively new for the twenty-first century, but what does this sound like? It's very similar to the stock market, where companies appeal to a public market to buy their stock in order to raise capital. The problem with Kickstarter,

GoFundMe, and other crowdfunding sites is that the relationship is still debtor and creditor. The debtor is now owing back many creditors a small amount instead of one big creditor of a large amount. Most times, these crowdfunding sites don't even have a means of paying people back, so they are marketplaces of people voluntarily giving their money from the goodness of their hearts without expecting anything in return.

I had a childhood friend, Jacob, who was diagnosed with stage IV angiosarcoma on his twenty-first birthday. He was completely healthy up until that point and used to be on the water polo team in high school. Jacob was enrolled at an Ivy League university, but his future plans of becoming a software engineer were put on hold when he was diagnosed with cancer. I remember seeing his crowdfunding campaign, which described his horrible predicament. I was shocked and saddened when I realized how quickly someone's life could change. On top of that, the inability to afford possibly life-saving treatments was a deeply startling notion to me (Kaplan, 2017).

We should not have to do this. It's clear that the health care system in America is completely broken. Until we get "Medicare for All," there will be more sad stories out there like Jacob's. It shouldn't happen, but millions of people in America already experience these horrific medical emergency stories, which puts them into crushing debt. Crowdfunding is a Band-Aid solution to a bleeding wound that will not stop flowing until it is fixed. Until that time, we can only work with the tools we have. For many people, that means raising money through friends, family, and kind strangers from the internet.

So far, we've discussed some ways through which people can get out of debt in our current human institutions. Now, let's discuss a marketplace that doesn't yet exist. Instead of creating an online campaign, Sam learns about a new marketplace where people can invest in him—like in the stock market—and if he turns his situation around, then his value will increase. When Sam's value increases, then the people that invested in him also benefit. This win-win marketplace where people can invest in each other is made possible through cryptocurrency.

Sam's stock in this case would be a digital coin that is connected to his worth. Usually, this happens for people when they become very rich, and a large institution wants to value their net worth. Sam, on the other hand, is not super rich—in fact, he is the opposite. Creating a coin and promoting the investment to his friends and family would raise the money Sam needs to get out of debt. Through that process, all his investors would also see a value appreciation of Sam's coin. They will feel good about helping Sam in his time of need and get rewarded for making a good investment in the long run.

Moses Finley, the great classicist, once said:

"There was basically one revolutionary program throughout antiquity: Just cancel the debts and redistribute the land, in that order" (Talks at Google, 2012).

Debt is both a tool and a trap. It is up to the individual to not let this tool trap them into perpetual debt. Many Americans are already trapped in debt and as the quote above implies, we need to figure out a way to change our current system or we will continue to repeat the historical cycle of revolution and redistribution. A new system to tackle debt should not be debt-based at all but investment-based. With cryptocurrency a new world of possibilities is becoming a reality. We can make credit and debt systems obsolete and replace them with investment systems where everyone can benefit in a win-win marketplace.

PART 2

CRYPTO-CONSCIOUS

CHAPTER 5

Money in Politics

___

THE HISTORY OF MONEY IN POLITICS

Cryptocurrency has the potential to disrupt everything, including politics. For hundreds of years, the American political process has remained largely unchanged in any fundamental way, as intended by the Founding Fathers. The twenty-first century and the invention of the internet commenced a new wave of politics that was more fast-paced, open, and transparent, whether politicians liked it or not. Cryptocurrencies offer a paradigm shift for people hoping to bring a balance to the current power structure.

The United States is a representative democracy, meaning that voters elect politicians to represent them. Having a political system that focuses on two primary parties—Democrats and Republicans—is a big problem, as it allows money to be the primary influence for both parties. Money from wealthy donors, corporations, and lobbyists flows into politics and allows their interests to supersede those of average American citizens.

According to a study by Anne Baker called "Getting Short-Changed? The Impact of Outside Money on District Representation": "Unfortunately, the results suggest donors can incentivize members to adopt more ideologically extreme positions that are in keeping with donors' ideological preferences. In doing so, the donor class successfully gains surrogate representation while leaving constituents short-changed when it comes to the quality of representation they are likely to receive from their members of Congress."

The main problem is that the will of the voter is being ignored and replaced with the will of the donor. It takes a lot of money to run a successful political campaign—millions and millions of dollars. That money is not free, either; there are strings attached. These strings are often at odds with the will of the average American citizen. When politicians eventually win their elections, the donors come asking for things that will help their bottom-line. This pay-for-play system creates a political vacuum that enables bribery and corruption.

David Hawkings is the editor in chief of *The Fulcrum*, a nonprofit and nonpartisan news site that is dedicated to covering problems that threaten the US democratic system. He is the leading editorial voice in creating the first digital news platform focused exclusively on the issues that have broken American democracy and efforts to make governments work again, in DC and across the country. *The Fulcrum* is a not-for-profit organization with total journalistic independence and a commitment to helping voters decode the dysfunction, understand why it's threatening our national future, and get involved in fixing the problems.

David Hawkings simply explains the fundamental problem of money in politics: "Money is essentially unregulated in the system now. And it is flowing not just toward the candidates themselves but onto the TV, radio, and the [internet], at a really high rate of speed. It's unfettered, it's unregulated, it's undisclosed in many cases. And this has all happened at a highly accelerated rate in the ten years since the Supreme Court essentially took the brakes off. [The Supreme Court] said corporations, unions, and rich people all have a First Amendment right to spend as much as they would like to influence the outcome of elections.

Hawkings continues, "The spending has gone up almost exponentially in the last ten years, depending on how you measure it. And really what that means is that the small-dollar donors, even the people who want to get involved and put their oar in financially, those small-dollar donations that most Americans, that if they want to give at all, that can afford to give $25, $50, $100, or their entire community could afford to give, wouldn't come close to the amount one billionaire could give" ("Preserving a Strong Democracy," 2020).

David Hawkings repeatedly mentions that the Supreme Court decision on January 21, 2010, of Citizens United v. Federal Election Commission (FEC) resulted in a fundamental shift in how money can be used in politics. The case started two years prior when Citizens United, a non-profit organization, wanted to promote a film for Hillary Clinton's campaign for presidency. The limits of how much money a corporation could contribute to an election were covered in The Federal Election Campaign Act (Martin, 2010).

Basically, the Supreme Court decided that a corporation's free speech was protected by the First Amendment right to free speech. Nowhere in the actual First Amendment does it specify that corporations are given the right to free speech, but now, they have the same rights as people. This essentially makes corporations the same as people in the eyes of the law.

The Citizens United Supreme Court decision may go down in history as one of the most infamous in how it has challenged our democracy and free speech rights. In just ten years, we've already seen the consequences, as trust in the government plummeted to a low of 20 percent, down from 30 percent, according to Pew Research Center. The amount of money spent by political action committees (PACs) skyrocketed to $4.5 billion over the decade versus $750 million in the two decades prior (Evers-Hillstrom, 2020). Lastly, politicians vote against the will of their constituents 35 percent of the time (Schechter, 2017).

We're in need of a fundamental change within the system behind money in politics. Organizations like Wolf-PAC and American Promise are actively lobbying states to pass a constitutional amendment to overturn Citizens United. So far, twenty-two states have passed resolutions in support of passing the Twenty-Eighth Amendment. We need to reach thirty-eight states before it becomes law, and we can start to rebuild this broken system (Liston, 2021).

Cryptocurrency offers a new way for politicians to raise money and not rely on their wealthy donors who contribute to campaigns with strings attached. There are also crypto-currencies that offer a new way to govern without the bribery and corruption of our current system. In the sections ahead, I'll explain these new and exciting solutions.

MONEY IN POLITICS TODAY

My first exposure to politics as a voting-age adult was back in 2016, during the US presidential election. I remember feeling inspired after listening to presidential candidate Bernie Sanders talk about progressive policies and the reason behind his campaign to become president.

I had the pleasure of hearing Bernie speak at a rally in Santa Maria, California. I remember being so excited for his vision of the future and the policies he supported, like Medicare for All, a Green New Deal, and getting money out of politics. He is a trailblazer in US politics, and his candidacy was revolutionary in how he challenged the political and Democratic establishments.

As a new voter, I was learning about the political process for the very first time. Some things that I found out really shocked me, like how much money it takes to build and run a successful campaign for president. Even more shocking was how each candidate raised those funds.

Bernie Sanders was the outsider of that race in 2016. As the longest serving Independent in Congress and new candidate running to be a Democratic party nominee, he was taking on the entire Democratic establishment. The amazing part of his campaign is that he put his money where his mouth was and only accepted donations from grassroots organizations and individual contributors.

Traditionally, candidates will spend most of their time raising money through wealthy donors and PACs, which is how corporations and special interest groups funnel millions of dollars to politicians who represent their interests. It's rare in politics for a candidate, of any kind, to reject this fundraising model and instead build a movement of many individuals who each donate a small amount.

Bernie was the first to run for president using this contrarian model, which allowed his message to be heard by millions and his movement to grow across the nation. Bernie's campaign raised over $200 million from 2.5 million individual donors, with an average donation amount of just $27 ("Sanders, Bernard—Candidate Overview," 2021).

I co-founded the Bernie Sanders for President Club at my university, Cal Poly, San Luis Obispo. It was amazing to see the support for a progressive president on campus and throughout the community. In the San Luis Obispo County presidential primaries, Bernie Sanders beat his main opponent, Hillary Clinton, in part because of the grassroots campaign we built there. Unfortunately, Bernie did not beat Hillary to become the Democratic nominee, but nevertheless, his movement inspired millions to run similar grassroots campaigns across the United States.

The next generation can now build off the revolution Bernie Sanders started to challenge the political establishments, just like how Bitcoin is an inspiration for people to challenge the financial establishments. Cryptocurrency and politics are more related than you might think.

One of the key characteristics of cryptocurrency is that you don't need a central authority like the government to control it. So why not use cryptocurrency and blockchain technology to govern? This idea is still in the beginning stages of development, but there's already been a lot of major progress.

Jeffrey Berns is a multimillionaire and founder of Blockchains LLC. In 2018, he announced the beginning of a ten- to fifteen-year journey to build the first smart city that is completely powered by blockchain. The governor of Nevada called this 67,000-acre smart city an "innovation park." The utopian-like vision that led Berns to fund this venture is truly inspiring and gives me hope when thinking about all the issues we still need to address as a society.

Berns plans to build the first ever esports arena inside the smart city. Nathaniel Popper from *The New York Times* reported, "The business side of the city will feature 'a highly secured, high-tech Blockchains Campus that joins blockchain technology with artificial intelligence (AI), 3D printing and nanotechnology,' according to the design firms." This smart city will showcase all the amazing potential blockchain has to offer in one place.

Imagine being able to cast a vote using blockchain as easily as an app on your phone instead of going to a physical polling location or voting early by mail. Pete Martin, CEO of Votem, a company that deals in blockchain voting, is working on making this idea a reality. Blockchain can quickly verify votes without needing to rely on poll counters, which leave room for human error ("Blockchain Voting," 2021).

This also solves the chain of custody problem, which is that when you leave your ballot in a mailbox, you essentially lose custody or possession of your ballot (Pressgrove, 2020). So many antiquated problems with our current election process need to be addressed, or we're doomed to repeat them. The future is bright with blockchain technology solutions to problems we face today.

THE FUTURE OF MONEY IN POLITICS

Money in politics is at the core of all political problems because it leads to corrupt and donor-biased politicians who frequently vote against the will of the people. Solving this issue is a big priority that will lead to change across the political system.

Challenge Coin is going to address money in politics by making the process of campaigning more transparent and more accessible to a majority of Americans. If donors want to give money, then they'll have to do it through the blockchain, where it's on the public record. Also, all contributions will be made by people, not corporations and PACs, through this new system, so everyone who contributes will be on the same playing field.

Challenge Coin will fundamentally change the relationship between politician and voter so that there's a direct relationship between the two. Poll numbers may have been a metric for politicians in the past, but their coin's value will be the metric of the future.

Let's take Bernie Sanders for instance. In order to get the grassroots support he needed, Bernie had to get tens of thousands of donations from people averaging $27 a piece. With Challenge Coin, Bernie would create his own cryptocurrency, called Bernie Coin, where he would ask people to invest in his coin.

The main difference between the two systems is that with Bernie Coin, people are investing, not donating their money. I donated $30 to Bernie Sanders' campaign in 2016. If I had invested in his campaign, then it would have given me more motivation to help Bernie win. Grassroots campaigns are the future of politics and changing the nature of campaign contributions so voters can financially benefit will lead to greater political involvement. People would be incentivized to support their candidate by canvassing and making phone calls as well.

Engagement in politics would skyrocket if regular people could actually make money while supporting their preferred candidates. The American Presidency Project reports that, in the twenty-first century, the average voter turnout for presidential elections of voting age adults is 55.62 percent. Most people don't vote because there's nothing in it for them except frustration and disappointment. They need a reason to get involved and investing in politicians as a way to crowdfund campaigns is the fundamental shift we need.

Now let's pretend that Bernie Sanders actually became president by fundraising through Bernie Coin. As president, you don't really have a direct way of seeing how your actions impact your constituents. Bernie Coin does not stop capturing value once Bernie Sanders gets elected. His first one hundred days in office would lead to more people investing in Bernie Coin if they liked what policies he was passing. If the value of Bernie Coin started to drop during his presidency, Bernie would know that he has lost touch with his constituents and needs to realign with the will of his voters.

The value of favorability could be captured as a president, which would make running for re-election an easy process. The need for wealthy donors and PACs would become obsolete as the politicians now have the tool that they didn't know they needed to connect with their voters. With Challenge Coin, every politician can launch a grassroots campaign to fund their run for office.

If your voters do not like what you're doing as a politician, then you can pretty much guarantee that people would sell any of those politicians' coins that they invested. That direct feedback, from let's say an issue that the politician voted on, would lead to a change in behavior. If the politician doesn't change, then they would not have enough funds to win re-election.

That fear of being voted out is the traditional way through which voters give politicians feedback every two or four years. There's nothing currently stopping an elected official from lying to their voters and then doing whatever their wealthy donors want once they're done campaigning. We need to establish a way to hold politicians accountable throughout their term so that they aren't tempted to vote against the will of the people.

The relationship between voter and politician would be stronger if the politician's coin was used as a tool to keep them accountable throughout their term. If a politician makes a campaign promise and never delivers or does the opposite, then the voters have to wait till the end of that politician's term to vote them out. Alternatively, if the politician upsets their voters, then the value of their coin would fall, making them more likely to appeal to their voters sooner.

Challenge Coin will fundamentally change politics for the better. It is a technology that allows politics to operate on pace with social change in the twenty-first century, and it also offers a solution to the plague of corporate funding in politics. The relationship between politicians and voters needs to evolve if we are ever going to repair the harm done by the Citizens United Supreme Court decision. Corporations are not people and do not deserve the First Amendment right to free speech. Our democracy is being bought and sold by wealthy donors and PACs that represent corporate interests.

There are a few options available to address money in politics: We can pass a constitutional amendment to repeal Citizens United. If that doesn't happen, then there are blockchain solutions to make the election process more transparent and accessible. Lastly, there's Challenge Coin, which could fundamentally transform the relationship between politician and voter.

CHAPTER 6

Entrepreneurship and Raising Money

———

THE ENTREPRENEURSHIP STRUGGLE—RAISING MONEY
Jeff Desjardins is the editor in chief of Visual Capitalist, a media site that creates and curates visuals on business and investing. He said:

"Statistically speaking, there is over a 50 percent chance that any new business is toast in five years. And the record for tech startups? It's even worse, with 90 percent of all startups eventually failing."

New businesses fail at alarmingly high rates, and the cause of that failure can be connected to cash flow or the lack of it. Jeff Desjardins explains:

"One study by US Bank shows that 82 percent of small businesses fail because of cash flow mismanagement. This is a fair point, since without cash flow, there is no business."

I studied business administration with a focus in entrepreneurship at Cal Poly, San Luis Obispo. My love for entrepreneurship grew when I was an officer for the Cal Poly Entrepreneurs club. I met some amazingly inspiring people who were all passionate about what they were working on. I enjoyed helping these entrepreneurs with their business needs and money was often at the forefront of the conversation.

In an article by Laura Entis, a reporter for *Fortune's* Venture section, she explains that "only 0.91 percent of startups are funded by angel investors, while a measly 0.05 percent are funded by VCs 'Venture Capital.' In contrast, 57 percent of startups are funded by personal loans and credit, while 38 percent receive funding from family and friends."

When an entrepreneur is just starting out, there aren't many ways to raise money. Typically, they will reach out to their friends, family, and followers for financial support. This type of fundraising is called the 3F's in Silicon Valley, except historically, the third "F" stands for "fools"—fools because most startups eventually fail, statistically, so they would have to be a fool to invest in one.

Self-funding is a very common way that entrepreneurs finance their companies when starting out. This could mean funding with actual money that the entrepreneur has saved up. Taking out bank loans and/or maxing out credit cards is sometimes necessary to keep the startup afloat. Also, sweat equity is another way entrepreneurs can run their startup without taking a salary. The reward for the entrepreneur working, essentially for free, is the value of the equity in the company.

Crowdfunding offers a new avenue for entrepreneurs to raise capital online. It's an effective way of building an audience around the idea for the product/service before incurring any big upfront costs. Being able to gain traction online and then launch the startup is a relatively new funding option for entrepreneurs. The investor in this case does not get any equity stake in the company. Rather, the investors are early adopters who get delayed gratification from helping get the company off the ground, and in return, they receive early access to that startup's product/service.

When all these opportunities for raising money have been exhausted, entrepreneurs can then pitch their startup to wealthy investors. Angel Investors are usually successful entrepreneurs themselves who want to give back to the next generation of entrepreneurs. Since most startups fail, the Angels aren't always motivated to make a return on their investment. Sometimes they believe in an entrepreneur or startup idea and just want to see them succeed.

Venture capital (VC) firms are the apex predators of raising money. They will invest millions of dollars into startups but only if they can get a 10x return for their portfolio. Andreessen Horowitz, also known as a16z, is a very popular VC in Silicon Valley that has invested in companies like Lyft, Facebook, and Airbnb. They even have a "Crypto" portfolio of over twenty-five companies like Coinbase and MakerDAO. These investments were millions of dollars, and a16z is often successful at finding these unicorn, $1 billion valuation startups.

An unlikely way entrepreneurs raise money is through government grants. These grants are designed to incentivize certain types of startups to exist. For example, the Small Business Administration has grants for entrepreneurs who are military veterans and for businesses that are environmentally focused. It's not common but great for those who can get funded this way because the government doesn't take an equity stake for the grants they award.

After the startup has been successful for long enough and wants to get to the next level, then another way to raise money is an initial public offering (IPO). An IPO is the process of a startup becoming a corporation, with shares of stock being offered to the public. It's like crowdfunding, but you need a bank to evaluate your business before it can enter a public exchange. An IPO is a great way to raise millions of dollars by selling millions of shares to banks, businesses, and individual investors.

Entrepreneurship is a risky business, which most often leads to failure. Elon Musk was lucky to have had so many startup successes, but even he had some close calls in his career, as we'll see in the next section. The importance of raising money and cash flow for businesses is crucial to their overall success. So now that we have a general understanding of the ways in which entrepreneurs can raise money, let's look into some stories of entrepreneurs today.

ENTREPRENEURSHIP—THE STRUGGLE TODAY

Elon Musk is generally recognized as the Tony Stark of our time. In January 2021, he briefly surpassed Jeff Bezos as the richest man alive with a net worth of approximately $184 billion, after Tesla stock rose 720 percent in 2020 (Klebnikov, 2021). He has founded many companies including Tesla, SpaceX, SolarCity, Hyperloop, and Neuralink. Elon's journey to the top was met with many financial hurdles, including almost losing everything he had worked so hard to build.

From humble beginnings in South Africa, Elon was a child-hood prodigy who learned to code at the age of ten. At twelve years old, he coded his first video game and sold it for $500 (O'Kane, 2015). After graduating from University of Pennsylvania with a BS in economics and a BA in physics, Elon moved to Silicon Valley in 1995. He founded a tech startup called Zip2 during the internet boom of the nineties. Elon says, "The funding we raised for our first company came from a small group of random angel investors in Silicon Valley" (Strauss, 2017). Eventually, Zip2 was sold to Compaq in 1999, for $307 million (Hull, 2014).

Elon personally made $22 million from the sale of his first company, which he then used to self-fund his next startup, X.com (Hull, 2014). There was a pattern of successful business acquisitions that led to Elon benefiting financially and then using that wealth to fund his next ventures. Fast forward to 2008, the financial crisis, when Elon was CEO of both Tesla and SpaceX. Both companies were on the brink of bankruptcy, and Elon used all the money he had to keep them afloat. SpaceX's first three launches had failed, and Elon had to scrape together enough money for the fourth launch, which luckily succeeded. Tesla was in the middle of a financing round that barely went through on Christmas

Eve in 2008; the alternative outcome was bankruptcy (Oli-varez-Giles, 2013).

In 2021, Tesla and SpaceX are tremendous successes, and Elon has continued to start companies that will change the world for the better. Elon's opinion of Bitcoin started off, in 2019, as cautious, saying that he was "neither here nor there on Bitcoin" but also commented on there being illegal trans-actions on the platform (Shevchenko, 2020). With the price surge of Bitcoin in 2021, Elon said that he would want to be paid in Bitcoin and that "a future Mars economy could be based on cryptocurrency, such as Bitcoin" (Bambrough, 2021). While Elon's opinion of Bitcoin continues to change, the cryptocurrency community is actively working to get Elon to see the future potential of this technology.

My journey learning about cryptocurrency started during my senior year of college. In early 2018, I was in an interview for a business internship with a tech startup, Unanimous AI. The CEO, Louis Rosenberg, asked me what topic I'd be most interested in: sports, cryptocurrency, or the stock market. I told him cryptocurrency, and that was the beginning of the crypto rabbit hole I would eventually go down, culmi-nating in this book. Louis is one of the smartest people I know with over 350 patents to his name, and in a TED Talk, he explained the brilliant idea behind his startup ("Louis Rosenberg," 2021).

Louis graciously agreed to be interviewed about that time when the Bitcoin bubble was at its peak and everyone, includ-ing him, wanted to be a part of it. His startup, Unanimous AI, is an artificial intelligence company that uses AI to connect groups of people together to amplify group intelligence. Their technology and methods are modeled on the biological principle of swarm intelligence, which is nature's method of harnessing and amplifying the intelligence of large groups. Swarm intelligence is why birds flock and fish school and bees swarm. They are smarter together.

The swarm technology works, and Unanimous AI can make groups of people significantly smarter. They are able to make significantly more accurate predictions, forecasts, estimations, decisions, and prioritizations. Louis explained that Unanimous AI was looking into cryptocurrency in three ways: initial coin offering (ICO), forecasting cryptocurrency prices, and rewarding quality forecasters with a token.

An initial coin offering (ICO) is similar to an IPO, except instead of shares of stock, companies sell their coin to the public. This coin is not a stake in the company but an early investment in that company's currency, which may or may not increase in value (Sherry, 2019). ICOs currently have little to no regulation, so there are a lot of scams to watch out for if you are looking to invest. The Security and Exchange Commission (SEC) has taken action against companies with fraudulent ICOs and companies that do not register with the SEC when releasing their coins to the public ("SEC.gov— Cyber Enforcement Actions," 2021).

Louis explains his thoughts behind not doing an ICO for his startup: "There was this big surge of fundraising efforts using Bitcoin because it was a new frontier. It was unregulated, and then the government started regulating it. It basically spooked a lot of companies from pursuing that anymore.

Then right around the same time, or not long after that, the price of Bitcoin crashed, and the price of cryptocurrencies crashed. So most reputable companies decided to sit back and wait, and not try to raise money through a coin offering."

Even though the "new frontier" of ICOs was intriguing, after talking to brokers and lawyers, Louis decided, "It just seemed too risky because the rules of the game, the rules of the road, weren't clearly written by the government. And so, you just didn't know if you were going to do something and then have the government come back later and say that what you thought was a legal way to raise money, was not. Or make some other change after the fact that you couldn't expect."

The other interest that Louis had in cryptocurrency was forecasting prices using swarm intelligence. Unanimous AI has successfully forecasted many things, from the Kentucky Derby Superfecta to Presidential elections, by amplifying the intelligence of professionals in those spaces. I joined the team with the intention to forecast prices of cryptocurrencies. Soon, we learned that the market was too volatile and the cryptocurrency enthusiasts we recruited were not knowledgeable enough to predict the extreme fluctuations of the crypto market.

The last way that Louis sought to incorporate cryptocurrencies to his startup was by creating a token to reward quality forecasters. Louis remarks, "We do forecasting, and we care about rewarding good participants and incentivizing participants." The idea was to have an ecosystem of forecasters who would be paid in Unanimous AI's token for making accurate predictions. This project ultimately did not take shape, but Unanimous AI was just one startup of many that were looking at Bitcoin and cryptocurrencies as an opportunity to raise more money and reward their users with currency that was specific to their company's ecosystem.

When I asked Louis what he thought about the future of blockchain and cryptocurrency, he theorized:

> *Whether you're trying to create a currency or need to track any other value but want to do it in a way where it does not require a centralized corporation to control it, or central government, or central bank, blockchain is a pretty remarkable solution.*

Louis continues by stating:

> *Personally, I think that's where there's going to be this endless Gold Rush because it is a fundamental change in what's needed to assign and track value, even for something as simple as just tracking how many followers a person has [on social media]. With cryptocurrency, you could do that without a centralized corporation being in charge. And that's attractive to a lot of people who worry about the power of corporations or worry about the power of central banks.*

FUTURE OF ENTREPRENEURSHIP

Both Elon Musk and Louis Rosenberg have struggled with cash flow for their startups. The reason I was laid off at Unanimous AI was due to financial constraints and lack of funding from venture capital firms. These financial hurdles are part of the entrepreneur's journey. I remember in my Entrepreneurial Finance class in college the analogy of an entrepreneur driving a car: the car is their startup, and they have to make it to their next destination on the gas, or resources, that they have. Most entrepreneurs run out of gas and never make it to their destinations.

In an ideal world, cars would be electric, like Tesla, and they would be able to get much farther than we currently can on old-fashioned, gas-guzzling vehicles. Cryptocurrency is like the electricity that powers the electric vehicle startups in more ways. Instead of relying on a gas station, or venture capital firm, entrepreneurs can fund their startups through the internet, which in this analogy would be the Sun. The Sun is the ultimate renewable energy source, and we have just begun to imagine ways to tap into it. ICOs are risky and unregulated now, but that does not mean we should stop thinking of ways to use electricity to tap into the Sun and fuel us to our future destinations.

The future is still being written, so it's up to us to imagine the best possible one and make it a reality. There is a special place in my heart for entrepreneurs who are doing everything they can to will their visions for the future into existence. I hope to develop a new way to help entrepreneurs get the resources they need to arrive at their next destinations. My idea for Challenge Coin is to create a cryptocurrency that would allow entrepreneurs a new way to fund their startups.

Elon Musk is a serial entrepreneur, and if he had started his entrepreneurial journey with his own coin, tied to his worth, then who knows how much more he could have accomplished. Let's say Elon Coin would have been created when Elon started his first internet company. He could build an audience around his first venture, and the success of the startup would drive the value of Elon Coin even higher.

By investing in Elon Coin, you own the success of Elon Musk over his whole entrepreneurial career. Traditionally, people can invest in a company and all their return on investment comes from that company's success or failure. With Challenge Coin, investing in the entrepreneur is the best of both worlds. If the entrepreneur's startup succeeds, then the investor in the entrepreneur's coin succeeds, and if the startup fails, then the investor experiences a temporary dip until the entrepreneur works on their next venture. The investor in Elon Coin would already be invested in all future ventures that Elon Musk has started in his lifetime.

I believe Louis Rosenberg and many entrepreneurs have the same potential as Elon Musk to succeed. Challenge Coin can help a generation of entrepreneurs raise money for their startups without the hurdle of relying on venture capital firms or other traditional ways of raising money.

If Louis Rosenberg had created Louis Coin when he started Unanimous AI, then he could see the value of his coin grow with every success of his startup. Imagine the day when Louis won a $20 bet on the Kentucky Derby Superfecta back in 2016. The bet was to predict the first four horses in order from first to fourth place, out of twenty total horses. They turned that $20 into almost $11,000 by swarming horse enthusiasts to amplify their intelligence as a group. That event received a great deal of media attention, which could have driven the sales of Louis Coin ("Swarm Intelligence Nails Kentucky Derby Superfecta, Turns $20 into $11,000," 2016).

Independent of the value of the startup, Louis gave a TEDx Talk in 2017 titled, "New Hope for Humans in an AI World." That video got over half a million views, which could have been another opportunity for people to invest in him, through his coin. People want to be a part of the next big thing, and for entrepreneurs, being able to capitalize on that could mean the success of their startups.

I plan on being the first entrepreneur to try this new funding method as a way to raise money for my startup, Challenge Company. The first challenge I will be tackling are the inequities of the economy by creating Challenge Coin. Ethan Coin will be the first coin created in this new economy. People will be able to invest in me, my ideas, and my future ventures by buying Ethan Coin.

The ultimate goal is to empower a generation of entrepreneurs by creating this new cryptocurrency economy. The saying "a rising tide raises all boats" applies perfectly to the elevated entrepreneurs who will hopefully be able to accomplish even more with the ability to fund their startups with an individual coin (Kennedy, 1961). The entrepreneurs' coin will raise money for them throughout their entrepreneurial journeys and careers.

CHAPTER 7

Influencers and Followers

WHAT IS AN INFLUENCER?

What's something Marilyn Monroe, Michael Jordan, Gary Vaynerchuk, and Taylor Swift all have in common? They are all influencers with millions of loyal fans and followers. This chapter will analyze the relationships of influencers and followers while offering a glimpse into the future of this relationship.

Influencer Marketing Hub describes an influencer as someone who has: the power to affect the purchasing decisions of others because of their authority, knowledge, position, or relationship with their audience, as well as a following in a distinct niche, with whom they actively engage. The size of the following depends on the size of their niche topic.

Influencers are people who can affect the behaviors of their followers. Influencers can include musicians, authors, celebrities, entrepreneurs, politicians, Thought leaders, religious leaders, CEOs, actors, inventors, sports stars, famous people, TV personalities, and more. These people influence their respective fields in many ways.

Influencer is a term that is used to describe people with a large online following. The internet and social media have made the relationships of influencers and their followers, or fans, more connected than ever. Before the internet, the relationship between an influencer and their followers was far less connected, as we'll see in this section.

INFLUENCING, PRE-INTERNET

Back in the 1950s, Marilyn Monroe was at the height of her career. She was a movie star, fashion and pop culture icon, a renaissance woman, humanitarian, and so much more. Marilyn won a Golden Globe for Best Actress in a Comedy in 1960 for the movie *Some Like It Hot*. In 1962, she tragically died from a drug overdose in her Los Angeles home ("Marilyn Timeline See All," 2018).

Marilyn Monroe said, "And if I want to say that the people, if I am a star, the people made me a star. No studio, no person, but the people did." Marilyn knew the level of stardom that she had reached was because of her fans and the people who watched her movies, read magazines of which she was on the cover, and followed her life. She didn't take the positive relationship she had with her fans for granted. She even cut her honeymoon with Joe DiMaggio short to entertain one hundred thousand US troops in South Korea for ten days (O'Hara, 2015).

The main way Marilyn Monroe benefited financially from stardom was through film studios. In 1954, Frank Sinatra was set to earn $5,000 a week compared to Marilyn's $1,500. Fox Studios wouldn't even let her read the script to the movie *Pink Tights*. Marilyn used her influence to challenge the decision makers at Fox. Her staged scandal involving nude photos actually increased her brand and forced Fox Studios to accept some of her demands (O'Hara, 2015).

Marilyn Monroe faced many challenges as a rising movie star. The film industry did not respect her and wrote her off as a "dumb blonde." Marilyn worked hard to make a name for herself and eventually created her own film production company because the studios had most of the power in the transaction. Marilyn had a lot of influence over her fans and was able to use her power to make changes in the film industry (Kettler, 2017).

Michael Jordan is in the basketball Hall of Fame for being one of the best professional basketball players of all time and a member of "The Dream Team." He won multiple MVP awards and carried the Chicago Bulls to the NBA Championships five times. Michael's rise to stardom was not only limited to playing basketball. He was the star of the movie *Space Jam* and used his brand to start a Jordan branded shoe with Nike (NBA, 2010).

I watched an ESPN Docuseries called *The Last Dance*, where I felt like I was teleported back in time to the nineties, when the Chicago Bulls were on a hot streak. With Michael Jordan as their all-star, the Bulls won six NBA championships between 1991 and 1998 with two three-peats. It was amazing to watch these games for the first time, since I hadn't been born until the end of 1995. Michael's competitiveness and true determination to win was spectacular to see on the basketball court.

Michael Jordan's basketball success led to $94 million in total playing salary, and in 1998, his final salary with the Bulls was over $33 million. He went on to own the Charlotte Hornets, start a tequila brand, and earned an estimated $1.3 billion from Nike for his shoe brand. He's made another $1.7 billion for endorsing brands and products like McDonald's, Gatorade, and many others. Michael Jordan's total net worth is $2.1 billion, according to *Forbes*. It is clear that Michael Jordan has greatly benefitted from his hard work, success, and brand.

However, the real beneficiaries are the institutions and gatekeepers behind Jordan's brand. Nike made over $3 billion by selling Air Jordans in one fiscal year ending in May 2019. Thanks to the success of *The Last Dance*, Nike's Air Jordans had over a billion dollars in sales in just one quarter in late 2019. The Chicago Bulls franchise value in 2020 is $3.2 billion despite not having won a championship since 1998, when Michael Jordan was the star player. These organizations are the ones capturing most of the value of Jordan's relationship with his fans (Badenhausen, 2020b).

The lives of Marilyn Monroe and Michael Jordan are like many other influencers across different disciplines. Before the internet, organizations held most of the control and benefited the most from the relationship between influencers and their followers. They became the middlemen who captured the financial value of fans through merchandise, branding, and general consumerism.

Michael Jordan said, "I hope the millions of people I've touched have the optimism and desire to share their goals and hard work and perseverance with a positive attitude" (Western, 2021). Michael knew the impact he had on his fans, including their mentality toward life and achieving their goals. Challenge Coin would allow Michael to influence millions of people who strive to be better, and that intangible value is still not being captured today, not by Nike nor the Chicago Bulls.

In the next sections, we'll explore how the internet and social media have disrupted these power structures. Then, we'll discuss how cryptocurrency could make any "middleman" obsolete when it comes to the relationship between influencers and followers.

SOCIAL MEDIA AND THE RISE OF THE INFLUENCER

The internet will go down in history as one of the most powerful tools of all time. The printing press allowed for the sharing of information at scale, but the internet goes a step further by connecting the world at scale and speed.

Social media is a new phenomenon that connects tribes of people all over the world. Communities on Reddit exist for things as obscure as "r/anarchychess" and get thousands of followers. But as the saying goes, "With great power comes great responsibility" (Cronin, 2015). Technology giants like Facebook, Apple, Google, and Twitter have more power than many countries with their abilities to influence masses of people (Gross and Manjoo, 2017).

After watching the Netflix documentary, *The Social Dilemma*, I realized the importance of putting a check on the power of these tech giants. Even though not all observers agree with the film's analysis, there is value in the relationship we have with one another, and companies like Facebook are extracting most of the value for their own benefit. The consumer has become the product when using social media through targeted advertising and behavior manipulation. In order to break free from the control of social media companies, we must take back the value of our connections and relationships with our followers, friends, and fans (Orlowski, 2020).

The following are some successful social media influencers who are currently using the tools at their disposal to deliver and create value within their online communities.

Gary Vaynerchuk started off as a wine connoisseur within his family's wine business and quickly learned of the power of internet marketing, online communities, and building a brand. He scaled his family's business from $3 million to $60 million in sales by creating WineLibraryTV on YouTube in 2006 and trying different wines to engage his followers. With an eye toward the future, Gary branched out to create his own marketing agency, VaynerMedia (Vaynerchuk, 2021).

Now Gary is a five-time *New York Times* best-selling author, influential public speaker, host of a global top 100 business podcast, successful angel investor, and chairman of VaynerX, a media-communications holding company. The list of accomplishments and ventures is even longer, but the theme of Gary's success is how he treats his fans. Gary elevates his audience because he believes that when his followers succeed, he succeeds (Vaynerchuk, 2021).

During my pre-order campaign for this book, I tweeted @garyvee, and within minutes, he responded by saying "Cheering for u" and "Go go go." It was one of the highlights of my campaign but also a testament to how Gary engages with his fans.

Gary Vaynerchuk's belief that his followers' success is his success is true, except he doesn't realize how true it actually is. Cryptocurrency is the missing link that brings value to both influencer and follower alike.

My friend Sam Betesh is someone I got to know in college, and I found out that in addition to being housemates, Sam was an internet celebrity. On YouTube, Sam goes by XJawz, and he has hundreds of thousands of followers and millions of views for his *Call of Duty* videos. Brands like Microsoft and Sony would sponsor XJawz in order to get their products mentioned in his videos.

Sam was an early YouTube influencer, but he had aspirations to do more than that. In college, he started a company called BrandPlug to connect influencers with sponsorship opportunities. He later moved to Los Angeles and continued to work in the influencer space. This time, he started a company called BoringRevenue to help clients by tapping into a network of micro-influencers.

These are influencers but at a smaller scale, like those who have less than one hundred thousand followers. Micro-influencers are the next evolution of social media marketing, since people engage more with them compared to mega-influencers who have around a million followers or more. According to The State of Influencer Marketing 2020: Benchmark Report, "The ratio of mega-influencer to micro-influencers rose from 1:3 in 2016 to 1:10 in 2019. In other words, there are now ten micro-influencers for every mega-influencer, compared with three micro-influencers per celebrity in 2016."

When I spoke to Sam Betesh for this book, he talked about the importance of trust between influencers and followers:

"There's a separation happening between influencers people trust and influencers people don't trust because of all the brand deals happening and influencer marketing going on. Consumers are deciding who they do and don't trust based on what products they promote." Essentially, when any influencer puts their name behind a product, they are staking their reputation on it. Cryptocurrency can capture the value of trust between influencers and followers, as we'll see in the next section.

Kyle Kulinski is a New York native and host of *Secular Talk*. Ever since my introduction to politics, I have found Kyle's commentary on current events to be liberating. His show is an affiliate of *The Young Turks*, a progressive news network, which is an alternative to mainstream media like *CNN* and *MSNBC*. This wave of alternative news is only possible because of the internet, which gave new media sites a platform to reach a global audience.

Both Kyle and *The Young Turks* face a new problem that influencers who talk about news and politics also face: censorship. YouTube is a fantastic platform because it allows influencers to get paid based on an advertising algorithm. YouTube's algorithm pays Youtubers based on how many views their video receives, the number of clicks an ad gets, subscriptions on their channels, and other factors. *Forbes* estimates that the average YouTube pay rate is $5 per one thousand video views. So, a million views could make YouTube influencers $5,000 on average (Mint, 2021).

The problem is that YouTube censors certain topics and programs on its platform that are more controversial, like

Secular Talk, and adjusts their algorithm so that advertisements don't appear on those videos, which means influencers that rely on revenue from their videos make less money (Kulinski, 2016). A solution to this problem that Kyle and other influencers have flocked to is Patreon, a membership platform that makes it easy for artists and creators to get paid directly from their followers. At the time of this writing, Kyle has 4,002 subscribers and makes around $13,000 a month from this platform (*"Secular Talk* with Kyle Kulinski Is Creating News & Political Commentary," 2021).

Taylor Swift is a famous singer-songwriter with many accomplishments in her career, including over two hundred million records sold worldwide, ten Grammy awards, thirty-two American Music awards (the most wins by an artist), and many more. When she first started out, Taylor asked a famous music producer what she should do to become a famous singer. He said to find one thousand true fans who would listen to and buy her music. Taylor Swift, determinedly, met with each person who listened to her perform live, and over time, with hard work, built a fanbase large enough to propel her career forward ("Taylor Swift," 2021).

"One thousand true fans" is a concept developed by futurist and author Kevin Kelly. He explains, "A true fan is defined as a fan that will buy anything you produce. These diehard fans will drive two hundred miles to see you sing; they will buy the hardback and paperback and audible versions of your book; they will purchase your next figurine sight unseen; they will pay for the 'best-of' DVD version of your free YouTube channel; they will come to your chef's table once a month. If you have roughly a thousand true fans like this (also known as super fans), you can make a living—if you are content to make a living but not a fortune."

One of the roadblocks to influencers benefitting from their one thousand true fans is that they do not have a direct relationship with their fans. They must capture all their support, unlike the small percentage they might get from a music label, publisher, studio, retailer, or other intermediary. Taylor Swift learned this the hard way in 2019, when her music had been sold to a company owned by a shady music manager. In order to regain ownership of her music, Taylor has to re-record her first six albums. Taylor now produces her own music, which allows her to have complete ownership while also maintaining a direct relationship with her fans ("Taylor Swift," 2021).

Situations where influencers must take on their intermediaries, like Taylor Swift with her music label, are why cryptocurrency is the perfect tool to aid in that power shift. Now influencers can finally keep all the reward from their relationship with their followers. But even more importantly, which we'll discuss in the next section, followers will be able to benefit from their relationship with influencers in a new way that hasn't existed until cryptocurrencies came around.

FUTURE RELATIONSHIP OF INFLUENCERS AND FOLLOWERS

So far, we've talked about the time before the internet and how influencers like Michael Jordan and Marilyn Monroe benefitted from their stardom. The real beneficiaries were the organizations that acted as intermediaries or gatekeepers to the influencers, e.g., studios, franchises, companies, etc.

Then, we discussed the internet and social media marketing, which gave influencers a global reach. Tech companies also expanded their reach and have greatly benefited from the online relationship between influencers and followers. Gary Vaynerchuk and Taylor Swift are just a couple of the millions of influencers online that are now able to make a living from this new era. Lastly, Sam Betesh delved into micro-influencers and the next wave of influencing people in niche online tribes.

I think that everyone falls into the category of influencer and follower in some way. For the most part, everyone meets people and connects on social media and slowly gains a following. You don't need to be a famous celebrity to be an influencer; in fact, we're all at the very least micro-influencers. I think it goes without saying how we are all followers—even the influencers follow people.

Challenge Coin is a coin that is connected to the value of a person, including influencers and followers. Let's say Taylor Swift had her own coin, which she could use as a way for her fans to buy her music, merchandise, and other Taylor Swift branded products directly. She could eliminate the middlemen that have gotten in her way because she does not need them anymore. Taylor Swift Coin is the tool that gives her the freedom and power to be independent from greedy music labels.

The beauty of Taylor Swift Coin is that, for the first time, Taylor's fans can do more than consume her content. They can invest in Taylor Swift by buying her coin. Now that there is a direct and reciprocal relationship with Taylor and her fans, she can finally unlock the true potential of her stardom. Taylor's true fans already buy her records, merchandise, concert tickets, and share their enthusiasm for Taylor all over the internet. Fans have never been rewarded financially for their part in building Taylor's brand, but soon, they will be.

Kyle Kulinski from *Secular Talk* needs platforms like YouTube in order to make a living. Since YouTube acts as the intermediary between content creators and advertisers, YouTube holds all the power in who gets paid. That has forced people, like Kyle, to move to platforms like Patreon to get subscribers/followers to pay them monthly for the privilege of seeing their content. In my opinion, this form of crowdfunding is not going to be enough for all influencers on the internet unless the subscriber becomes the investor.

We need to change the dynamic of the fan, who is a subscriber or consumer of the influencer's content, to an investor in the influencer's future potential value. This change creates a new cryptocurrency market for investment in people that has never existed before. Since everyone is either a(n) (micro-) influencer or follower or both, this market would far surpass the value of the stock market, which is just a collection of publicly traded companies.

The combination of the new dynamic between people where we all benefit from each other's collective success through investment and a market of collaboration that rivals the stock market, is an exciting proposition.

People are already acting in ways that are indicative of a cryptocurrency market of peoples' coins. Social media posts update followers on things going on in the influencer's life. Popular posts are engaged with likes, comments, and sharing, which would lead to a larger audience and reach more fans who could buy their coin. True fans would promote their favorite influencers to their friends and persuade their friends to invest in the influencer's coin. That coin appreciates in value based on the demand, which means that the fans are being rewarded for their contribution to the coin's increase in value.

My idea for Challenge Coin has many use cases, but the potential for tapping into the influencer and follower relationship is by far my favorite. Digital influencers are a relatively new phenomenon, and we're still trying to figure out the best way to capitalize on this connection. Cryptocurrency is a new opportunity, and not only do influencers benefit, but so do their followers. The only parties that lose in this transaction are the powerful status-quo managers of established industries who have played intermediary between influencers and followers for far too long.

I'll end with a quote from Gary Vaynerchuk about how he treats his fans like they're his legacy:

"I am acutely aware that my legacy is more about what my community creates than what I create because the scale in which that potential lies is far greater than any one man.... What fascinates me is my community. To be honest, I think my real legacy is you."

CHAPTER 8

Your Coin: The Life Cycle

———

HELLO, WORLD!: YOUR COIN IS CREATED
"Hello, World!"

This is the first thing a developer learns to code. Most coding languages start off this way, and cryptocurrency is no different (Langbridge, 2014). This chapter is going to be structured a little differently than the ones prior. Instead of a past, present, and future model, I'll be taking you through the life of your coin, which starts not on the day you're born, but the day you become a legal, voting-age adult.

When you turn eighteen years old, you are now able to open a bank account and enter legally binding contracts. It's appropriate that you would also be able to create your own smart contract in blockchain at that age. Since this birth story doesn't actually start the day you are born but the day your own cryptocurrency is created, I thought it would be fitting to title this section "Hello World."

To quickly recap, I am describing an idea that does not exist yet but hopefully will in the future. The idea is called Challenge Coin, which is a cryptocurrency that allows people to create virtual coins that will be connected to their personal worth for their entire lives. The life cycle of your coin starts whenever you want, once you turn eighteen, but it ends when you die (possibly).

When you create a coin, the process might look similar to opening a bank account. You need to verify your identity so that you can only create one coin for yourself. Once that is confirmed, you will be able to customize your coin's preferences. Preferences may include things like what metric of value to track (i.e., income, charity, investments), what do you want to happen after you die (i.e., coin ends, continues tracking legacy, distributed to your heirs), public or private, and other big life decisions, which I will explain in the following sections.

I want to pause here to note that this is hypothetical, which means that even though I have conceptualized these preferences and other thought experiments, the reality may be very different. So, I would appreciate it if you would indulge me in my thought experiment. It's important that as the reader you keep an open mind but also contemplate how this idea could impact your life.

A PERSON (AND THEIR COIN) IS UNIQUE

People are unique, and I don't think a coin tracking someone's worth should be standardized as a one-size-fits-all approach. It makes more sense to give individuals the power to decide how their worth should be measured. If you take the analogy of this idea being a stock market for people instead of businesses, then you are probably thinking that businesses have standardized metrics for tracking value like the P/E, earnings per share, quarterly and annual revenue, and other profit-driven metrics.

That's what I am trying to avoid, in all honesty. I think having an organization whose sole purpose is to generate more profits every quarter is non-human. People are diverse, with many factors that drive them. Maybe there are people who are money-motivated and that's how they want their coin to measure their worth; that will be their decision to make.

Having a tool that is flexible to the uniqueness of the individual also means giving the person the power to decide why people should invest in them. Are they going to make a positive impact on society through charity and volunteerism? Do they want to elevate the people around them? Are they happiness-seeking and just want to live their life without worry? I think all the above and combinations of other motivations are where the true value of a person lies.

PUBLIC VS. PRIVATE COIN

Back to the stock market analogy, every company in the stock market is a public entity. They offer shares to the public and have to report to their shareholders annually. This would be true for choosing to have your coin open to the public market as well. You would have the choice of deciding when to report to your investors. This process is similar to elected officials who have become public servants. We hold them to a higher standard because they are public personas who represent the people.

When you decide to go public with your coin, you are essentially agreeing to be held to a higher standard because you have investors who elected to support you with their investment. I hope that people take this obligation as seriously as being a public servant because that would lead to a better society of people who act ethically every day. Not all public servants are honest actors, but that should be reflected in their coin's value, incentivizing them to be better.

The alternative option is for you and your coin to remain private. The main difference here is that other people cannot invest in your coin until you are public. There's no funding mechanism while you are private, but you can invest in other people's coins. This preference is perfect for people that aren't ready for the responsibility of going public but still want to be a part of the ecosystem and benefit from investing in others.

Explained differently, in the stock market, the companies that go public are invested in by people and other entities that are not public organizations. So, what if someone decides to go from public to private? I imagine that, like stocks, the person would have to buy all their coins back so that they have no more investors. No investors, no more crowdfunding, and no more public coin.

A key difference between this idea and the stock market is that only people can participate in this new economy. Wall Street consists mainly of wealthy people and businesses who are constantly competing for more profits. To have a more equitable playing field, I think this dynamic needs to change. If only individuals can compete, not businesses, then everyone has the same twenty-four hours in the day to increase the value of their coin. It becomes unfair when CEOs can build organizations where they are at the top and extract most of the value from their workers, who don't see the same returns on their labor.

YOUR COIN AND YOUR EDUCATION

For the rest of this chapter, I'm going to assume that at the age of eighteen, you created your own coin, and it is public. The personal motivations that you decided to track throughout your life are both financial and impact-driven. You decided to define impact as the number of people you have positively impacted and the quality of that impact.

Congrats! You have applied to some colleges and were admitted to a couple of them. You start to realize that college is more expensive than you thought, and you might need to take out student loans. In the US, there are forty-five million borrowers who collectively owe over $1.5 trillion in student loan debt. On average, that's over $32,000 per student after they graduate from college (Friedman, 2020). As stated in the previous chapter on debt, millions of students are stuck with student loans for most of their lives after they have graduated and filing for bankruptcy doesn't make those loans go away, either.

This challenge of paying student loans is a big one for many Americans and for new students who have to decide how to pay for their education. Lucky for them, and you, there is a new way to raise money for your life goals, and it doesn't require you to go into debt for the foreseeable future. You created a coin with the goal of paying for college and furthering your education.

The next step is similar to a crowdfunding campaign, like Indiegogo and Kickstarter. When you create a campaign, you are asking for people to support you, and in return they get something like a perk, early access to a product, or another early adopter benefit. When you create a coin, you also need to garner the support of the early adopters who believe in you and want to see you succeed by being able to afford college. Most likely, these early investors will be part of the 3F's of entrepreneurship: friends, family, and followers/fans.

Let's say your family has saved some money for your college expenses. That money could be directly used on those expenses, or they can buy your coin, which essentially allows you to pay for those expenses, if you wish, and your family gets the added bonus of being early investors in your coin. As the years go by and you advance in your education, the value of your coin also increases based on the demand, depending on how your coin's value is being measured.

So, if your coin was worth $1 initially and your family bought $1,000 worth of coins, then the value grows to $2, then $4 and eventually $10, etc. That means your family is doubling, quadrupling, and eventually making ten times the amount they initially invested for doing the same thing families usually do to support their students. The key difference is that everyone benefits in the transaction except for student loan lenders, who have put generations of students into debt.

Another example of a way you can use your coin is through side projects. I remember that I was very involved in extra-curriculars like my entrepreneurship club in college. Many of the student entrepreneurs I worked with would start a cool side project with their friends and hit a roadblock when it came to getting funds to pay for it. Some colleges are great at offering scholarships and grants to support their innovative students, but that's not enough.

Students who experiment and use college as a way to challenge what is possible should be supported more broadly. Having your own coin while in college could mean more than just paying tuition but showing the world the things that you're working on while you're getting an education. Giving students a platform to showcase their successes inside and outside the classroom is a revolutionary concept that I hope empowers generations of students to dream big.

ADULTING—YOUR COIN'S VALUE GROWS

Yay! You graduated from college with no student debt, and now the world is your oyster, as the saying goes (Bell Team, 2021). The future possibilities are endless, but now you have to figure out what's next. Will you get your first job and move to a new area? Do you want to take time and travel? Maybe there's a charitable and fulfilling opportunity like the Peace Corps that awaits you.

At this stage of your life, your coin becomes an even more powerful tool because all the supporters that have invested in you so far are still rooting for your future success, however you choose to define it.

Let's say you choose to begin your career and join the working world. You're probably financially motivated with the goal of a better quality of life and more power/influence. If you decide to go down this path, then you'll inform your shareholders that's how they should calculate your success. If after a couple years you get a promotion and move into a nicer place, then the value of your coin would reflect your upward trajectory.

Another interesting concept is how you will be getting paid by your employer. Just like how your parents bought your coin to fund your college expenses, your employer could buy your coin to pay for your labor. This fundamentally changes the relationship between employer and employee. It essentially makes everyone a consultant, managing their own time and energy. Nine-to-five workdays may become obsolete because people have the freedom to take their most valuable asset, time, wherever they choose.

I love this thought experiment. I don't know if you can tell, but something as simple as giving people the power of their own life, through cryptocurrency, has these amazing ripple effects. Employers, like Amazon and Walmart, have all the power when it comes to hiring and firing people and paying them less than living wages. If you change the nature of the relationship from employer to investor, then people now have more ways to make a living.

Let's go back to the post-college thought bubble of what's next. Traveling the world is many people's dream, especially after they graduate college. I have many friends who have gone on some amazing trips only to come back to reality and find a job because they were running out of money. If you had a coin that made money for you while you were traveling, then you wouldn't have to "come back to reality." In my vision for the future, the reality is that you can fund your travels via cryptocurrency.

Your shareholders meeting version two might go like this: "I have an exciting announcement! I graduated from college and now I want to travel the world for at least a year. Attached is my tentative itinerary, and I hope you'll follow along and support me in my adventures. I could not have gotten where I am today without my supporters and just want to let you know how grateful I am to all of you. If you are near any of the cities I plan on visiting, let's hang out. I would love to connect with my top supporters, who made my dream of traveling the world a reality. Thanks again!"

In return for their support, you can offer to meet up with people while you're traveling. You could also start a travel blog and offer recommendations for people when they travel. Maybe you are volunteering abroad, and people want to support you for being so charitable. There are so many ways people provide value in the internet era, and having your own coin unlocks all the potential that life has to offer.

YOUR COIN'S VALUE MATURES

Eventually, you might decide to settle down in a place and call it home. Let's explore some more common life decisions that would be impacted by this new cryptocurrency concept. Some of the biggest life decisions that impact people financially are:

Getting Married: *This leads to divorce half the time— divorce drains an individual's wealth by an average of 77 percent, and that goes for both men and women.*

Buying a Home: *There are over fifty million Americans with mortgage loans lasting thirty or more years—the total housing debt in the US reached an all-time high of over $10 trillion (Fontinelle, 2021).*

Having Children: *American families spend between $10,000 to $25,000 on each child every year, from birth until they turn eighteen (Roos, 2013).*

Having your own coin should be a tool for each of these big life choices. Cryptocurrency isn't an asset that the government can steal from you. I don't think that a divorce would legally lead to half of the value of your coin going to your significant other in a settlement. But there's no regulation for cryptocurrencies at the moment, so it's hard to say how that might play out.

Having your own coin makes banks obsolete because you are essentially your own bank. I foresee a new type of loan industry emerging that invests in people who want to buy a house because they see homeowners as safe investments, just as banks do. Again, the main difference is that you aren't in debt to your investors. It's possible that there's a hybrid approach where you take out a loan from a bank but pay for that loan by crowdfunding your coin.

Lastly, children: the reason we're all here is because our parents, and their parents, and so on, all decided to have kids.

Is having your own coin reliable enough for you to support your family? That is a tough question and I want to say yes, but honestly only time will tell. The best I can do is remind you that the US dollar only buys 15.55 percent of what it could fifty years ago because of inflation. Since the decoupling of the gold standard, the problem has only gotten worse. You would need $643.15 to buy the same goods you'd buy for $100 back in 1971 ("$100 in 1971 → 2021 | Inflation Calculator," 2021).

Therefore, the real question is, can you afford not to find an alternative to the US dollar? Bitcoin may be the reliable option, and other cryptocurrencies may become the next world reserve currency after the US dollar. Here is an ambitious statement: If enough people from around the world participate, then Challenge Coin could be the next world reserve currency. The idea of everyone having their own personal cryptocurrency, collectively, makes up the entire global population. The US dollar only represents the economic value of the US economy which is not representative of the world in any way.

The only reason the USD remains the world reserve currency is that the US government and military is so powerful that no other country's currency could replace it. Well, Bitcoin and other cryptocurrencies are independent of governments' influence, and that is why it makes sense that the next widely adopted cryptocurrency could become the world reserve currency. Challenge Coin is the platform that will enable individuals to create their own currencies. I believe that Challenge Coin has the potential to become the world reserve currency because it would reflect the total world economy.

An economy is simply a collection of people's transactions. People are the fundamental building block of all human institutions. Governments and countries represent the people they govern. Companies are people working together toward a common goal. Schools are people teaching each other. When you think about the world this way, then you will start to understand why this idea is so powerful.

Empowering people with cryptocurrency and their own coin gives them the freedom to live life on their terms. The beauty of this idea is that everyone benefits through collaboration. Imagine how productive we can all be when we put our collective minds together to solve big world challenges. This tool may be the most important in order to unlock humanity's full potential for positive change and collaboration. And I am just getting started.

ALL-TIME HIGHS OF LIFE

What are some examples of an all-time high (ATH) of life? Some people say that their lives peaked during college, but that's not really true. Our lives go through many ups and downs, but I think the overall trajectory of a person's life is up. We are constantly growing every day. We learn new skills, meet new people, accumulate more wealth, and experience more things.

If we continue our thought experiment, then you might be wondering what this coin valuation might look like. This is an illustration I made that shows what it could look like to have a coin your whole life, from the time you were a legal adult until the day you die. You can see that your worth grows for most of your life. This could obviously be a different pattern for each individual, but speaking generally, I think most life value curves will follow this path.

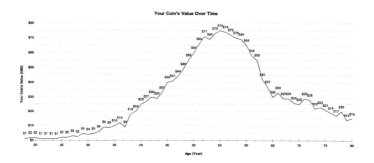

Your Coin's Value Over Time

Reaching an ATH in life, in this context, is when you have maximized your impact on the world, or own as much wealth as you can, or reach another ultimate life elevation that begins the natural declination of worth from your ATH. I see this time in a person's life as when they no longer need to keep growing because they have everything they could ever want or need. It's when you are content with the status quo and just want life to stay where it is.

I'm only twenty-five, so I'm guessing a little bit here, but I think we all hit a point in our lives where there isn't this urge for more. It changes to an acceptance of what is and what was. Parents may feel this when all their kids are grown up and have empty nests. People feel this when they have reached the top of where they want to climb and stay where they are at after a career of growing. When you finally buy something you've always wanted, like a house or car, and you're content with what you have.

This is an awesome time because you have finally made it. You achieved almost everything you wanted in life. Enjoy it! Go on vacation with your family. Travel the world with your loved ones. Keep putting energy into your fulfilling side projects. Do whatever brings you happiness because that's what the power of your coin gives you. After years of building a brand and a following of supporters, you can finally reap the rewards of wealth accumulation. Just like how the mega-rich get to live in their ivory towers at the top of the world, you can also enjoy all that life has to offer—maybe not at the same level, but you get the idea.

At this point in your life, when you have reached your all-time high, there may not be a need for raising capital to fund your life goals anymore. There is still an important function that you get to participate in, and that's investing in others. This can happen at any point in your coin's life cycle, but when you have more than what you need, that is when it's time to give back. The amazing part is that giving back also benefits you because you're not giving but investing.

Investing in the next generation is like planting the seeds for the future of humanity. Every generation of people has continued the progress of generations prior. A currency that is forward-thinking enough to empower future generations is one worth buying into. When the next generation needs money to solve their problems, you will be able to invest in their success, which then becomes part of your cryptocurrency's legacy.

That's the next gold rush. When I thought of this book title, I wasn't referring to buying Bitcoin, Ethereum, or even

Challenge Coin as the next gold rush. The next huge opportunity is to be able to invest in people, the most undervalued, underappreciated asset class. We all need to start seeing the value in each and every one of us because nothing would be possible today without people. People are the backbone of all great achievements, from space travel and other technologies to the Seven Wonders of the World.

There could be whole industries created around the new ability to invest in people, just like all the industries focused on Wall Street and the stock market: investment firms, financial advisors, stock traders, and more. There could be people that make it their full-time jobs to invest in people who are likely to grow in value.

The best investors would be similar to Warren Buffet, who is a value investor. Warren is one of the wealthiest men alive; he made most of his money by understanding the true value of a company, buying stock at a discount compared to his opinion on its real value. Back to cryptocurrency, if Warren were investing in people, I think he'd want to hold onto his investment for years because people grow over long periods of time.

There are so many implications for an idea this big, and I appreciate that you've indulged my thought experiment. Hopefully, I've addressed some of your questions about how cryptocurrency could impact your daily life. You probably have more questions that you're curious about, but all will be answered in time. The future is bright with possibilities, and Challenge Coin is one that I wish becomes a reality.

YOUR COIN AFTER DEATH

What happens after you die? It's the age-old question that has puzzled humankind for millennia.

Well, for Challenge Coin, it's simple: you died, so your currency will too.

There's no afterlife in the sense that your coin's value—which you've spent your whole life growing—doesn't keep existing once you've kicked the bucket. Instead, what happens is that your investors, your followers, get to keep their investments in your coin at the value when your life ends. That's the fairest outcome, where the people that contributed to your success are also the heirs of your worth after you die.

In a philosophical sense, the people that you touched while you were alive would also be the ones who have invested themselves in your success. That same love and support is being quantified by your cryptocurrency and distributed back out to the ones who supported you while you were living. I think it's a beautiful and symbolic analogy that feels right when you consider that for the first time, we can calculate a person's entire value with this technology.

I'm not a developer, but if this were technically feasible, I'd want this version of Challenge Coin to be built. With the innovation of smart contracts, another possibility is that you, the owner of your coin, have the choice to decide the outcome your coin's value after you die. Like a will, your inheritance would be up to you to decide who gets what. Maybe 50 percent of the value of your coin goes to your significant other and the other 50 percent goes to your investors. That would be up to the coin's owner to set up in the creation process of the coin when the smart contract's terms are set.

Another scenario is that cryptocurrency value does not end after you die. This would mean that, like Bitcoin, once a new coin is created, it is forever in existence. This option immortalizes peoples' coins and all their attributes (supply, inherent value) for all time. You could still invest in that coin even after the person dies because that person has created so much value in their life that it is still creating value after the person died. Your coin becomes your legacy, capturing the value you create even after you are no longer alive to do it yourself.

People have legacies today. Everything from your children, your business, and other impactful things that remain in this world long after you have died. It is possible that just like an artist's life, where their work becomes more valuable after the artist dies, a person's coin could also become more valuable as well. Tracking your legacy's value is not something that has been done before, either. Many interesting unintended consequences may come of it, but this is true for the idea overall, so it's best to experiment and see what works in real life.

PART 3

CRYPTO-CAPITALIST

CHAPTER 9

Warning: It's the Wild West

FULL DISCLOSURE

Even though I have enjoyed the process of researching cryptocurrencies and talking to crypto leaders, I am just an author with a big idea. I'm not a financial advisor and am not qualified to tell you how to invest your hard-earned money. I'm simply a curious person with an eye toward the future, and I invite you to also learn more about this exciting technology.

That being said, if you're reading this, then you are probably already aware of my qualifications but may not be aware of all the risks associated with cryptocurrencies. This chapter is designed to give you a healthy dose of caution before investing more than you're willing to lose, like your life savings, into something you might not fully understand.

THE WILD WEST OF BAD ACTORS

A bad actor is someone who is intentionally dishonest and unethical in how they conduct themselves. The opposite of a bad actor is an honest actor, who is someone who acts with honesty and integrity.

There are bad and honest actors in every facet of society. That's where the government comes in, to regulate industries and protect people from bad actors in all forms. Cryptocurrency is still a relatively new emerging technology that lacks regulation, and in most cases, the government can't regulate it even if it wanted to. This dynamic is similar to the 1800s, when people were more self-reliant and solved disputes as a community with little help from the government.

The Wild West was an era of cowboys, Native Americans, pioneers, outlaws, and gunslingers brought together for the purposes of expansion, greed, and a new frontier. Sound familiar? Cryptocurrencies have brought together developers, cryptographers, economists, and philosophers for the purpose of developing a trustless system that lacks a central authority, like the government. In these unregulated times, where the next frontier is ripe with opportunities, it's important to know the difference between real gold and fool's gold (Pak, 2020).

THE ART OF THE CON

Donald J. Trump was the former president of the US, twice impeached in Congress, with six businesses that went bankrupt. He is a pathological liar and one hell of a conman. Donald founded Trump University and scammed people with a fake school that had no accreditation (Duignan, 2021). He was fact-checked over the course of his four years as president and was found to have lied to the American people over thirty thousand times (Kessler, 2021). His lies ranged from lying about China paying for the border wall to the turnout of his inauguration and the suggestion that the 2020 presidential election was stolen from him, even though he claims he won by a landslide ("PolitiFact," 2021).

Con artists like Donald Trump have deceived people to get what they want since the beginning of time. In the nineteenth century, there were European entrepreneurs who sold false cures, or "snake oil" and deceived people in order to make money from them. The snake oil salesman would say that properties in the product he sold would have some unsubstantiated positive health outcome, like the ability to live a longer life or cure chronic ailments. We eventually learned to outsmart the ruses of these con artists, but the cons keep changing (Gandhi, 2013).

Cryptocurrency is a new technology that is still not fully understood by most people, so there's a new opportunity for con artists to take advantage of people. Richard Heart, the founder of HEX, is a perfect example of someone who has taken advantage of people in the crypto space. There are outspoken supporters of HEX, so I encourage you to do your own research, just as I have done.

The HEX website says that it is not a scam, and that HEX gets its value "through progress in replacing Gold as a store of value, Mastercard, Visa, and PayPal as payment networks, and CD's as time deposits. The market has decided that crypto currencies are worth hundreds of billions of dollars over many years of price discovery."

HEX is a cryptocurrency within the Ethereum blockchain ecosystem that claims to operate like a decentralized certificate of deposit (CD). When you buy a CD with a bank, the bank holds it for a specified period and invests your money, earning you interest. That's the business model of HEX, except there's no interest earned because there are no investments being made. The way the value increases is by controlling the supply and demand of HEX tokens so that they increase in value overtime.

The scam is that Richard Heart is able to manipulate the supply of HEX coins in his favor. When a HEX coin is staked or held for a long period of time, Richard can move the coins to his personal wallet and exchange them for another cryptocurrency, like Ethereum (ETH). It is important to note that not all cryptocurrencies are alike, so do your research before investing, especially if there are credible outlets calling it a scam (Southurst, 2020).

Con artists like former US President Donald Trump and Richard Heart come in all shapes and sizes. In both cases, many people were conned for their money, so it's important to be vigilant and ask questions. Does this business model make sense? Do I have control over my (crypto)currency? Are the people behind the company/cryptocurrency trustworthy? Am I willing to lose my money if I made a bad investment?

HACK ATTACK

With the rise of the internet, hacking has become a major problem for organizations and individuals. Hacking refers to the activity of identifying weaknesses in a computer system or network in order to take advantage of the system they are trying to infiltrate. The purpose of hacking can change depending on the hackers and what they want, which could include: access to secure networks, passwords, sensitive data, control of a system, or other lawless acts ("Potential Security Threats to Your Computer Systems", 2019).

These cybercrimes impact everyone, and it's important to take precautions to avoid being hacked and potentially losing your valuable digital data and currency. On July 15, 2020, over one hundred high-profile Twitter accounts were hacked, including those belonging to Elon Musk, Bill Gates, Jeff Bezos, Barack Obama, and many more. Hackers were able to use social engineering to get access to Twitter's centralized admin tools in order to change individuals' profiles.

These profiles said, "I am doubling all payments sent to my BTC address for the next 30 minutes. You send $1000, I'll send back $2000." Within hours, over $100,000 was stolen from hundreds of people who fell for this scam. I fear that the more widely adopted cryptocurrencies become, the more incentive there is for elaborate hacks like the one at Twitter to occur (Iyengar, 2020).

Another type of hack for cryptocurrencies is called a 51 percent attack. Basically, cryptocurrencies operate a network of nodes that decentralize the validation of new transactions. If a hacker is able to control 51 percent of the network by running a majority of the blockchain's processing power, then the hackers are able to send themselves currency through double spending. The more nodes a network has, the more costly it is to achieve this kind of hack (Wong, 2018).

Over the years, many cryptocurrencies have experienced 51 percent attacks including Verge, Ethereum Classic, Bitcoin Gold, and Vertcoin. Bitcoin Gold is a hard fork, or "spinoff," from the original Bitcoin blockchain. When that split occurs, most of the processing power behind the network follows the main blockchain, in this case Bitcoin. Having fewer nodes powering the Bitcoin Gold network leaves it more vulnerable to being attacked (Attah, 2019).

In May 2018, Bitcoin Gold was attacked, allowing hackers to manipulate the cryptocurrency. Exchanges like Bittrex, Binance, and Bitfinex lost an estimated $18 million worth of coins by exchanging fake Bitcoin Gold coins for other cryptocurrencies; this attack essentially undermines the integrity of the cryptocurrency that is being attacked. This is a real problem for new and smaller cryptocurrencies that do not have a big enough network to make an attack not worth the effort. According to Crypto51.App, it would cost an attacker $329 to rent the processing power to do a 51 percent attack on Bitcoin Gold for an hour.

There are many other forms of hacks to watch out for, like malware and ransomware, which are oftentimes accidentally downloaded on your computer by clicking a hacked link. Please be overly cautious when exploring the world of cryptocurrency, but also the internet in general. Double-check links you click on, use two-factor verification for your online accounts, and make sure you have a wallet that stores your cryptocurrency off exchanges.

PONZI, PYRAMID, AND MULTI-LEVEL MARKETING SCHEMES, OH MY!

You can get rich quick! Wanna retire in your thirties? I'm making millions, and you can, too, if you follow my ten-step plan to wealth and prosperity. You're only one click away from achieving your financial dreams.

There's a saying that if it's too good to be true, it probably is ("Something ... Encyclopedia.com," 2021). Another saying, if you smell a rat there probably is one ("I Smell a Rat - Meaning, Origin," 2019). All I'm saying is that you have to be on high alert when you are exploring new opportunities. Be careful and do your research because you do not want to be on the losing side of a scam or scheme.

The Con Artist Podcast defines a Ponzi scheme as "a redistribution of wealth, hiding behind a fake investment scheme. It takes money from new investors and hands it to old ones, meaning that the only way to pay old investors is to find more and more people to buy into the fraudulent system. Without a steady stream of new blood, the whole operation goes up in flames."

Charles Ponzi, from whom the phrase "Ponzi scheme" originated, was born in 1882 in Italy and became known in the 1920s as a swindler in the US and Canada for his money-making scheme. Charles saw an arbitrage opportunity for International Reply Coupons (IRC), which were postage used for international mail, priced at local postage prices. Charles realized that he could buy IRCs in one country, sell them in another, and profit the difference—at least, that's what he claimed to his investors (Zuckoff, 2005).

It was actually infeasible to run this scheme. For the thousands of investors who bought into the Ponzi scheme, there would have needed to be a Titanic-sized ship full of IRCs. When it eventually collapsed, Ponzi's investors were practically wiped out, receiving less than thirty cents on the dollar. Overall, they lost about $20 million in 1920 dollars, which is approximately $196 million today ("Charles Ponzi Biography," 2021).

Charles Ponzi is nothing compared to Bernie Madoff, who cost his investors about $18 billion, fifty-three times the losses of Ponzi's scheme. Bernie operated the largest Ponzi scheme in world history and the largest financial fraud in US History, worth over $64 billion. He took advantage of his status, reputation, and clients' trust to deceive thousands of people and take their money. Bernie confessed that his firm and its successes were "all just one big lie" (Quisenberry, 2017).

Bernie Madoff "stole from celebrities, billionaire investors, Holocaust survivors, athletes, and team owners. He stole from individuals and charities, retirement funds and nest eggs. He stole from his friends and family" (Murden, 2019). Around thirty-seven thousand people felt the devastating fallout from Bernie Madoff's deceptions. This scheme was perpetrated within Wall Street for decades and even survived multiple SEC investigations. If Bernie could get away with something so financially devastating for so long in a regulated industry, then it's no surprise that similar schemes could happen in the unregulated cryptocurrency space.

Let's examine what a cryptocurrency Ponzi Scheme looks like, so you don't fall victim to one. These crypto Ponzi schemes also rely on new investors to pay older ones. Bit-Connect was a cryptocurrency that promised returns that were too good to be true. They guaranteed that $1,000 would earn 1 percent daily interest if you exchanged Bitcoin or USD for BitConnect Coin. If this return was true, then your initial thousand-dollar investment would be worth more than $50 million in three years (Mix, 2018). Becoming a millionaire that quickly and easily is too good to be true in any context.

The next red flag is Multi-Level Marketing (MLM) style programs, which BitConnect utilized. MLMs, or pyramid schemes, require recruitment of new investors to build the wealth of the people above them. The person or people at the top of the pyramid benefit the most from this referral system, while the people at the bottom of the pyramid lose money or benefit very little. At BitConnect, most of the rewards came from affiliate commissions that drove up the demand of BitConnect Coins and their price.

The payout process of BitConnect is what makes it a Ponzi scheme. Users were locked in for a certain period in order to get the high yields promised by BitConnect. When you exchange Bitcoin for BitConnect, those Bitcoins are never returned. Instead, you receive more BitConnect coins when your loan contract is completed. In 2018, when BitConnect shut down some of its services after receiving a cease-and-desist order, the value of BitConnect nosedived by more than

90 percent (from over $400 to $17.25 per coin). People who were tied up in BitConnect coins lost millions of dollars (Higgins, 2018).

Investments like Ponzi schemes, pyramid schemes, and MLMs are not designed to make people money but to extract money from people to pay the creators and early investors of these schemes. Always be skeptical of investments that seem too good to be true and promise unrealistic returns. Do your research. Ask questions about unsustainable business models and do not assume that people who've invested in a Ponzi scheme are going to tell you the whole truth.

SCAMS AND SCHEMES

The amount of money lost to phone scams in the US in just 2020 was nearly $20 billion (O'Dea, 2020). The IRS phone call scam is a good example. Someone pretends to be from the IRS to get your social security number. Phishing scams where scammers pretend to be someone they're not in order to deceive people for their money are the most common. Email phishing is a serious problem, and many companies have created spam folders to collect all those phishy emails so that their users do not get scammed.

I personally went through an impersonation scam for my author Instagram account, "@ethan.turer.author." My sister told me that she got a weird message from me on Instagram. She knew it was weird because we don't normally communicate via Instagram direct messages. This fake Instagram account that was pretending to be me asked my sister how she was doing, to which my sister replied, "fine." After I was made aware of this impersonation account, I wanted to figure out what the goal was. Why me?

I found out that it's not hard to copy a social media account, including photos, bio, and the like. The thing they couldn't copy were my followers, but this account had a similar follower and following count to my real account, except all their followers were fake, too. Just by doing a little digging, I was able to figure out that their username was "@ethan_turer_ author." So, by using underscores instead of periods, they were able to deceive some of my followers into thinking they were me.

Luckily, I was able to stop the fraud from continuing by posting a disclaimer that I would never ask people to send me Bitcoin and to help me in reporting this fake account. The account eventually got taken down, and the people who were deceived did not lose any money because I tipped them off. This example is, unfortunately, the norm online. It is more common to encounter a scam because people can hide behind fake accounts and fake personas.

The more attention you get online, especially within cryptocurrency, the more you attract bad actors. They want to take advantage of your success and steal from you and your followers. Unlike credit card and bank scams, there is no way to reverse a crypto transfer, so it's even more important to be 100 percent confident where you send your cryptocurrencies.

FAKE COINS & WALLETS & EXCHANGES

Fake versus real can be hard to navigate in the Wild West of crypto. It's not that hard to appear credible on the surface, but once you look under the hood, you see the scam for what it is. Unfortunately, for most people, that means understanding the code that runs the network. I'm not able to do that, so I have to rely on the expertise of that cryptocurrency's community to find the fakers.

In the "Beware of These Top Bitcoin Scams" article, the #1 scam was fake Bitcoin exchanges. "In 2017, South Korean financial authorities and the local Bitcoin community exposed one of the most insidious Bitcoin scams: a fake exchange called BitKRX. It presented itself as part of the largest trading platform in the country and took people's money. To avoid this type of Bitcoin fraud, stick with popular, well-known Bitcoin exchanges and forums so you get news of fakes quickly" (Edmondson, 2021).

The #3 Bitcoin scam in that article was "fake cryptocurrencies": "A common scam is to present a new cryptocurrency as an alternative to Bitcoin. The idea is that it is too late to cash in on Bitcoin and that you need to invest in one of these up-and-coming cryptocurrencies. My Big Coin was shut down for this reason. The fraudsters behind My Big Coin took $6 million from customers to invest in the fake cryptocurrency and then redirected the funds into their personal bank accounts" (Edmondson, 2021).

The last fake scam to watch out for is hardware wallets. These are like personal bank accounts that store all your cryptocurrencies. Buying a wallet that has been tampered with could mean that someone else has access to your funds and can steal your money. It is important to buy from a trusted source, like Trezor or Ledger, and verify that you're the only one who has opened the package and saved your back-up seed phrase (Liebkind, 2020).

Remember that the hacks, scams, and schemes that are occurring in the cryptocurrency Wild West are not new. There have always been bad actors trying to take advantage of people and organizations. Since the cryptocurrency space is relatively new and unregulated, there are going to be growing pains like hackers and con artists trying to make a quick buck. Please proceed with caution. I hope that by being aware of these scams, you will not fall victim to them.

CHAPTER 10:

Investing in Crypto

INVESTING INTRO

"There's no such thing as a worry-free investment. The trick is to separate the valid worries from the idle worries, and then check the worries against the facts."

—PETER LYNCH

Just to reiterate, I'm not a financial advisor, guru, or Bitcoin billionaire. My investment knowledge and writings are for educational purposes only. Please do your own research.

When thinking about investments, there's a lot to consider. Whole professions and industries have formed to invest in all sorts of things, from stocks and bonds to foreign exchange and commodities. Cryptocurrency is a new speculative asset that has become popular because of the amazing price increases that have occurred in short time intervals.

Before I dive into crypto, I think we should take a step back and look at Wall Street for a better understanding of traditional investing. Then, we will see how cryptocurrency is similar but, in many ways, different so that you can see the whole picture before deciding to invest.

PAST: STOCKS AND WALL STREET

One of my favorite books about investing is called *A Random Walk Down Wall Street* (RWDWS): *The Time-Tested Strategy for Successful Investing* by Burton Malkiel. I'll be referring to this book a lot this chapter, so I highly recommend you check it out. There is even a section about the cryptocurrency bubble of 2018. The overall thesis of RWDWS is that investors who actively trade in the market are worse off than people who invest in an index fund for the long term.

> *"A random walk is one in which future steps or directions cannot be predicted on the basis of past history. When the term is applied to the stock market, it means that short-run changes in stock prices are unpredictable. Investment advisory services, earnings forecasts, and chart patterns are useless. On Wall Street, the term 'random walk' is an obscenity. It is an epithet coined by the academic world and hurled insultingly at the professional soothsayers. Taken to its logical extreme, it means that a blindfolded monkey throwing darts at the stock listings could select a portfolio that would do as well as one selected by the experts"* (Malkiel, 2020).

"All investment returns—whether from common stocks or exceptional diamonds—are dependent, to varying degrees, on future events. That's what makes the fascination of investing: It's a gamble whose success depends on an ability to predict the future" (Malkiel, 2020).

No matter how hard people try to convince you they can, no one can predict the future, not even Wall Street speculators. Timing the market is not something I advise, but many people do it, nonetheless.

There is an old investing adage:

"Time in the market beats timing the market."

Essentially, the efforts you could put into timing the market and trying to predict the future price of a stock, or any speculative asset, is better served elsewhere. Being invested in the market for long periods of time, including the dips, makes better returns than trying to avoid the dips (Litman Gregory Investment Team, 2020).

Crash recovery time

Even the unlucky people who invested $1,000 in the S&P 500 right before a stock market crash made their money back within a few years if they continued to add $1,000 to the market every year.

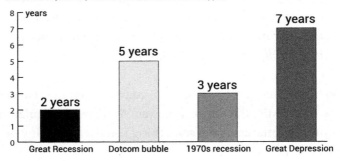

Let's look at this chart, which shows how timing the market looks in action. In 2008, the financial crash numbers showed that most investors sold when the stock prices fell, but by timing the market, they missed out on the 2009 increase in prices. A level-headed investor who stayed in the market would have made their money back in just two years (Egan, 2015).

Now that you understand the difference between timing the market and time in the market, let's explore how investors try to predict the future prices of speculative assets: technical and fundamental analysis. The easiest way to think about these two types of analyses is that technical analysis has to do with analyzing charts and fundamental analysis tries to understand the real value versus market price.

According to *Investopedia*, the goal of technical analysis is to analyze data, like changes in prices and historical returns, to chart patterns and find trends in order to estimate the future prices. Many chartists believe that the market is only

10 percent logical and 90 percent psychological. This philosophy suggests that predicting the market is essentially like predicting the behavior of groups of people.

The goal of fundamental analysis is to come up with a fair value of a company by evaluating all aspects of the business, along with the industry, the market as a whole, and the domestic and global environment. The fundamental analyst will evaluate the expected growth rate, dividend payout, degree of risk, and market interest rates, among other metrics (Horton, 2021). The key question is, do either of these analyses work for the individual investor?

Some of the greatest investors of our time have spoken to this very dilemma: "Even the legendary Benjamin Graham, heralded as the father of fundamental security analysis, reluctantly came to the conclusion that fundamental security analysis could no longer be counted on to produce superior investment returns. Shortly before he died in 1976, he was quoted in an interview in the *Financial Analysts Journal* as saying, 'I am no longer an advocate of elaborate techniques of security analysis in order to find superior value opportunities. This was a rewarding activity, say, forty years ago, when Graham and Dodd [were] first published; but the situation has changed.'"

Graham continues, "[Today] I doubt whether such extensive efforts will generate sufficiently superior selections to justify their cost…. I'm on the side of the [efficient market hypothesis (EMH)] school of thought." And Peter Lynch, just after he retired from managing the Magellan Fund, as well as the legendary Warren Buffett, admitted that most investors would be better off in an index fund rather than investing in an actively managed equity mutual fund. Buffett has stipulated in his will that cash from his estate be invested solely in index funds" (Malkiel, 2020).

The efficient market hypothesis, referred to above, outlines the theory that prices reflect all publicly available information in the market. Lucas Downey from *Investopedia* explains, "According to the EMH, stocks always trade at their fair value on exchanges, making it impossible for investors to purchase undervalued stocks or sell stocks for inflated prices. Therefore, it should be impossible to outperform the overall market through expert stock selection or market timing, and the only way an investor can obtain higher returns is by purchasing riskier investments."

So now that we have identified some of the losing strategies to making consistent returns in the market, let's discuss the time-tested strategies that have worked. Those timeless strategies from RWDWS involve broad diversification, annual rebalancing, using index funds, and staying the course. Each is a powerful tool to lowering risk, maximizing returns, and hedging losses.

Diversification is a risk management strategy which involves mixing a variety of investments in a portfolio. An example would be buying a mix of stocks and bonds in a portfolio. Stocks are considered to be riskier investments and yield higher returns, generally, while bonds are safer with consistent, albeit lower, returns. Broad diversification applies this same strategy by spreading out your investment among different markets and asset classes, e.g., stocks, bonds, exchange traded funds, real estate, venture capital, etc. Allocating your portfolio using broad diversification can help neutralize bad performing investments with good ones in the long run (Segal, 2021).

Rebalancing is another portfolio management strategy that mitigates risk. Let's say you are 60 percent invested in stocks, 20 percent in bonds, 15 percent in cash, and 5 percent in cryptocurrency. These percentages vary based on your risk tolerance and specific investing goals. If your stocks are doing exceedingly well, then the portfolio allocation may change due to the respective increase in value. Annual rebalancing would mean that every year, you adjust your portfolio to reflect the original portfolio you designed, in this case by selling stocks that are overpriced and buying bonds. This strategy is smart because it keeps your portfolio from taking on too much risk from excessive growth (Cussen, 2020).

Index funds are a portfolio of stocks or bonds designed to reflect the makeup and the performance of the broader market. The S&P 500 is a widely invested index fund which represents the top 500 companies in the US stock market. The idea is that you can diversify your risk by investing in a group of top companies with low management costs and benefit from the overall returns of the market. Instead of trying to pick the best companies yourself and taking on all the risk if they fail, an index fund picks a larger group of companies to match the return of the market (Fernando, 2021).

Staying the course is the last tool for investing but often the hardest in practice. In cryptocurrency terms, this is referred to as "HODL," or "Hold on for dear life." When volatility and price fluctuations eventually occur in any investment, are you going to hold onto or sell off your investments? In 2009, after the stock market collapsed, many people panicked and sold their investments because they did not want to lose any more value. The problem with this logic is that losses are not actualized until you take the action of selling. If you believe in your investment, then holding on allows you to recover from the paper loss when the investment eventually turns around. Those who held on during the 2008 crisis made their money back and more in a couple years. So, ask yourself, do you have the stomach to hold on during a similar crisis?

There are many more lessons to be learned about investing, but I hope the ones I described will provide clarity into the new world of investing in cryptocurrencies. These principles apply even more when deciding to invest in volatile, speculative assets with almost no regulation. As you will see, it's even more important to understand your risk tolerance and investment principles when you start to invest in Bitcoin and other cryptocurrencies.

PRESENT: CRYPTO

"Don't invest more than you can afford to lose and don't invest too much where you can't sleep at night."
—KENDY LAND, HOSTESS OF THE CRYPT KEEPERS' CLUB

If you've been asking yourself, "Wow, why is Ethan warning me about investing in cryptocurrency so much?" I am being honest and forthright about all the ways things can go wrong because I do not want my readers to be misinformed or lose any money. I want you to read this book and feel inspired about the positive aspects of this technology and be prepared for all the risks associated with investing in this space.

Bitcoin is the first cryptocurrency ever created. It is a break-through technology that allows people to transact without the need of a middleman keeping track. Bitcoin reached an all-time high of nearly $65,000 per Bitcoin in April 2021. What makes Bitcoin so valuable? Does Bitcoin have intrinsic value, like gold? The quick answers are 1) demand and 2) it depends, respectively, but let's explore the long answers (Kelleher, 2021).

All currencies need to be able to store value over time in order for them to be reliable. Since its inception, the value of Bitcoin has generally increased, which makes it a good store of value. As a comparison, the value of the US dollar has depreciated due to inflation, which makes it a bad store of value. Gold has typically been the store of value against fiat currencies, but many have foretold that Bitcoin may become digital gold for the digital world.

Depending on who you ask, the answer to "what's Bitcoin's intrinsic value?" could be very different. Some say that Bitcoin has no intrinsic value compared to gold, which is a precious metal with conductive properties. I believe, like many Bitcoin enthusiasts, that the blockchain technology that makes Bitcoin possible is intrinsically valuable. For the first time in the modern world, we are able to trust the blockchain to record our transactions and not a third party. There's value in the ability to trust a peer-to-peer network without needing a bank to hold our money for us. Trust is the intrinsic value that Bitcoin offers through blockchain technology (Kelleher, 2021).

The last point about Bitcoin's price reaching $65,000 is that there is a limited supply. There will only be twenty-one million Bitcoins ever created, which means it is scarce. Demand for the limited supply of Bitcoins drives up the prices to the levels we are seeing now. As long as there continues to be demand for more Bitcoins, the price will continue to go up. Luckily, one Bitcoin is divisible into one hundred million Satoshis, which allows for fractions of a Bitcoin to be used in everyday transactions (Kelleher, 2021).

"Bitcoin Maximalism" is the idea that Bitcoin is the only cryptocurrency that matters and that all the others are "shitcoins," or cryptocurrencies with no value or purpose. This idea is popular amongst the cryptocurrency community for a few reasons. First, Bitcoin has the strongest network, which may lead to a Bitcoin monopoly in the future. Second, Bitcoin's proven track record of reliability and success makes it the best digital currency. Lastly, Bitcoin is the best investment for a portfolio as all other shitcoins have not performed as well as Bitcoin. A Bitcoin maximalist's portfolio would only consist of Bitcoin and they would HODL until the whole world adopted Bitcoin and then say, "I told you so," until the end of time (Frankenfield, 2021).

Bitcoin prices have fluctuated wildly along with other cryptocurrencies. This price movement is too volatile for most investors. The best method for overcoming this volatility in cryptocurrency is by using a dollar-cost averaging (DCA) strategy. When you don't know whether the price is going to go up or down, DCA takes the guesswork out of timing the market. Instead of investing $1,000 at a given price, you spread out the investment over a specific interval. So, every month, you invest $100, which averages out the volatility of the asset. This low-risk strategy can be used with any amount for any interval you choose to invest in, so do what is comfortable for you and stick with it (Godbole, 2020).

You have finally decided to buy Bitcoin. How? Exchanges are a digital marketplace that allow for buying and selling of cryptocurrencies and other currencies. There are many exchanges to choose from, so for simplicity's sake, I will only refer to the most popular ones. Coinbase, Binance, Kraken, and Gemini are very popular exchanges that make it easy to buy cryptocurrencies. Open an account, verify your identity, and connect a payment method. Now, you are ready to buy your first Bitcoin. Each exchange charges fees for the convenience of buying through them, so do your research to avoid hidden costs (Frankenfield, 2020).

Now that you have your very own cryptocurrency, it is important to not leave it on an exchange, which is prone to being hacked. You can transfer your cryptocurrencies to digital wallets which are either hardware- or software-based. Wallets are like having your very own bank, which only you have access to. A software wallet, like MetaMask, is connected to the internet, which is called a "hot wallet" (hot meaning that it's riskier as hackers could still try to steal your crypto by getting access to your wallet through the internet). Hardware wallets (which look like USB drives), like Trezor and Ledger, are not connected to the internet and are referred to as cold wallets. If you are serious about investing in cryptocurrency, I recommend starting with a free software wallet and eventually buying your own hardware wallet to keep your investments safe (Frankenfield, 2021).

Keep in mind that maintaining your own crypto can be riskier if you do not understand how the technology works. User error is a lot more common off an exchange because there is no recourse for making mistakes like forgetting your seed phrase, sending crypto to the wrong address, and other common user errors. Please do your own research before making important financial decisions within the crypto space.

Other common questions investors ask themselves have to do with what to invest in. They know they want to have some cryptocurrency exposure in their portfolio, but they do not know which ones are the most worthwhile. There are not tried and true, widely accepted ratios and concepts for investing, like the ones that exist for stocks and bonds. However, some of the same principles can carry over nicely, as well as a few nuances that are particular to cryptocurrencies. Even though these choices are made at your own risk, the following might provide you with some good food for thought.

Cryptocurrency Evaluation Checklist

#	Category	Questions
1	Utility	• What's the mission of the cryptocurrency? • Does it satisfy a want or need that people have? • What makes this crypto different from all the others?
2	Leadership	• What's the leadership team like? • Do they have previous experience running a crypto project? • Do they seem fake or sketchy?
3	Country of Origin	• Where is it located/domiciled? • Is the country favorable to blockchain and digital currency? • Is there regulation of cryptocurrencies there?
4	Community	• How large and active is the community? • Do they have Discord, Twitter, Reddit, Telegram, etc? • Is the community full of bots and fake accounts?
5	Developer Activity	• How active are the code repositories that support it? • Is there a lot of innovation and development activity? • If not, does the project seem like people are losing interest?
6	Ease of Use	• Is the platform easy to use? • Does it still need a lot of work? • Is it something you would want to use regularly?
7	Investors	• Are investors pumping and dumping or HODL'ing? • Is the project well-funded? • How many whales (big investors) are there?
8	Supply	• How many wallets control the circulating currency supply? • What's the market cap? • Is there a supply cap or can infinite currencies be created?
9	Security	• What type of consensus does it have? I.e. Proof of Work/Stake • Are there a lot of validators/full nodes? • Has the network been hacked or 51% attacked?
10	Listed Exchanges	• How many exchanges is it listed on? • How easy is it for capital to find it? • Can you easily exchange your crypto for something else?

This checklist is a tool designed to help you evaluate any cryptocurrency. Let's go through an example together:

CRYPTOCURRENCY EVALUATION CHECKLIST: ETHEREUM

UTILITY
1. What's the mission of the cryptocurrency?
   a. According to Ethereum.org, the mission of Ethereum is to be the foundation for our digital future. The website says, "Ethereum is open access to digital money and data-friendly services for everyone—no matter your background or location. It's a community-built technology behind the cryptocurrency ether (ETH) and thousands of applications you can use today."

2. Does it satisfy a want or need that people have?
   a. There are six key features that most people want: banking for everyone, a more private internet, a peer-to-peer network, censorship-resistant, commerce guarantees, and compatibility across platforms ("What Is Ethereum?", 2021).
3. What makes this crypto different from all the others?
   a. Ethereum 101 states, "Ethereum is the world's programmable blockchain. It builds on Bitcoin's innovation, with some big differences. Both let you use digital money without payment providers or banks. But Ethereum is programmable, so you can also use it for lots of different digital assets—even Bitcoin! This also means Ethereum is for more than payments. It's a marketplace of financial services, games and apps that can't steal your data or censor you."

LEADERSHIP
1. What's the leadership team like?
   a. The Ethereum website does not have a page dedicated to the leadership team. Wikipedia may not be the most trusted source for this book, but there is a lot of great information from Ethereum's Wiki page, including the founders of Ethereum. According to blokt.com, in addition to Vitalik Buterin (the mastermind behind Ethereum), Ethereum Co-founders include Anthony Di Iorio, Charles Hoskinson, Mihai Alisie, Amir Chetrit, Joseph Lubin, Gavin Wood, and Jeffrey Wilcke.

2. Do they have previous experience running a crypto project?

    a. The eight co-founders of Ethereum have very interesting backgrounds, but not necessarily in running crypto projects. After looking each of them up on LinkedIn, here is what I found:

- Vitalik Buterin: Co-founder and writer at *Bitcoin Magazine*
- Anthony Di Iorio: CEO and founder of Kryptokit, founding member and executive director of the Bitcoin Alliance of Canada
- Charles Hoskinson: Founder of Bitcoin Education Project, founder of BitShares network
- Mihai Alisie: Editor-in-Chief and Co-founder of *Bitcoin Magazine*
- Amir Chetrit: Founder at Colored Coins
- Joseph Lubin: VP at Goldman Sachs, director at Blacksmith Technologies, and CEO at SyNerG Music
- Gavin Wood: Director of Technology at OxLegal, Technical Director at Lancaster Logic Response
- Jeffrey Wilcke: Chief Technical Read The Fucking Manual at StudyFlow, developer at MasterCoin (Sergeenkov, 2021)

3. Do they seem fake or sketchy?

    a. Ethereum was created in the early stages of crypto, so it is impressive that most of them had previous crypto experience. That being said, out of all the co-founders, only Vitalik is still actively working on Ethereum. Everyone else moved onto other projects. I do not believe any of them seem fake or sketchy, quite the opposite actually. They are clearly principled in their beliefs about the potential for blockchain technology.

COUNTRY OF ORIGIN

1. Where is it located/domiciled?
    a. According to Ethereum.org, the company was founded in 2014 and is based in Baar, Switzerland.
2. Is the country favorable to blockchain and digital currency?
    a. "In Switzerland, the government's general attitude towards cryptocurrencies, and in particular towards the technology underlying cryptocurrencies, is very positive" (Haeberli, Oesterhelt, and Wherlock, 2021).
3. Is there regulation of cryptocurrencies there?
    a. In Switzerland, cryptocurrency-related activities are not prohibited. Further, subject to the enactment of the DLT-Draft Law, there are currently no Swiss statutes or regulations that are tailor-made for cryptocurrencies" (Haeberli, Oesterhelt, and Wherlock, 2021).

COMMUNITY

1. How large and active is the community?
    a. Ethereum has one of the largest crypto communities in the world, second only to Bitcoin. This community also includes thousands of decentralized apps (DApps). The twenty-four-hour trading volume is $22,565,167,586 ("Ethereum (ETH) Price, Charts, Market Cap, and Other Metrics," 2021).
2. Do they have Discord, Twitter, Reddit, Telegram, etc.?
    a. https://ethereum.org/en/community/ This link has a list of many active online communities including Reddit, Forums, Discord, Twitter, and more.

3. Is the community full of bots and fake accounts?
   a. All communities at that scale will have some form of bots and fake accounts. The key is to figure out if there's proper moderation of those communities, and if not, then the community is most likely not real.
   b. Ethereum users are very real, and their communities have sufficient moderation to keep the community organic.

DEVELOPER ACTIVITY

1. How active are the code repositories that support it?
   a. Github.com is a popular site for developing crypto-currency projects. Kendy Land has developed a way to rank GitHub data for those projects. According to https://www.cryptkeepers.club/github-data.html, Ethereum receives an A+ for its amount of new GitHub activity.
2. Is there a lot of innovation and development activity?
   a. Mentioned previously, Ethereum 2.0 is a new upgrade that will bring the Ethereum network to the next level of scalability, security, and sustainability.
3. If not, does the project seem like people are losing interest?
   a. There is growing interest!

EASE OF USE

1. Is the platform easy to use?
   a. This is a more subjective question, but I believe Ethereum has many applications that can make it overwhelming for new users. Ethereum is a powerful tool and platform with many capabilities for DApps across different categories. The Ethereum website is easy to use and helpful for navigating this decentralized world.

2. Does it still need a lot of work?

    a. The transactions processed, energy consumed, and cost of the network need a lot of work. Ethereum 2.0 plans to address all these aspects in its upgrade, which should bring more scalability to the platform.

3. Is it something you would want to use regularly?

    a. I am using Ethereum regularly! I have MetaMask downloaded on my phone and use it for most of my cryptocurrency needs. Most DApps are in the Ethereum ecosystem, which makes it a popular cryptocurrency for daily users.

INVESTORS

1. Are investors pumping and dumping or HODL'ing?

    a. People have mixed answers to this question. Some claim that the big investors and developers are colluding to pump up the price of Ethereum. Others believe in the credibility of the network and are bullish about the future of Ethereum. It is possible both parties are correct, so it's important to do your due diligence.

2. Is the project well-funded?

    a. According to Cryptopedia, "Ethereum was also originally funded through an ICO, which took place in 2014. Buyers received ether in exchange for Bitcoin, and more than seven million ether was sold in the first twelve hours of the sale, worth approximately $2.2 million. By the end of the sale, more than fifty million ether were sold, amounting to about $17.3 million.

3. How many whales (big investors) are there?

    a. Cointelegraph Consulting says that the ten biggest investors only control 3.9 percent of the total ETH supply worth nearly $9.5 Billion.

SUPPLY

1. How many wallets control the circulating currency supply?
   a. According to Etherscan.io, as of June 18, 2021, there are 159,265,573 unique wallet addresses. Those are great numbers for a thriving cryptocurrency network like Ethereum.
2. What's the market cap?
   a. $257,809,802,673.52 ("Ethereum (ETH) Price, Charts, Market Cap, and Other Metrics," 2021). At the time of this writing, Ethereum is the #2 cryptocurrency in the world by market capitalization.
3. Is there a supply cap or can infinite currencies be created?
   a. Kendy Land, co-creator of the Cryptocurrency Evaluation Checklist says, "As I mention for supply of EVERY asset, ever—'The supply only matters as much as there is demand to outpace it. This is what determines price.'"
   b. There's no supply cap, but approximately eighteen million ether are mined, per year (Land, 2021).

SECURITY

1. What type of consensus does it have? I.e., Proof of work/stake
   a. Ethereum's website explains that proof of work has been the consensus protocol for Ethereum since its inception, but Ethereum 2.0 will transition to proof of stake protocol. The transition is planned to take place between 2021 and 2022.
2. Are there a lot of validators/full nodes?
   a. According to etherscan.io, there are 5,760 nodes running on the Ethereum network. Compare this to Bitcoin, which has around 9,000 nodes, according to bitnodes.io.

3. Has the network been hacked or 51 percent attacked?
   a. Ethereum has never been 51 percent attacked, but it has been hacked. According to Cryptopedia, "The DAO was a decentralized autonomous organization (DAO) that was launched in 2016 on the Ethereum blockchain. After raising $150 million USD worth of ether (ETH) through a token sale, the DAO was hacked due to vulnerabilities in its code base. The Ethereum blockchain was eventually hard forked to restore the stolen funds, but not all parties agreed with this decision, which resulted in the network splitting into two distinct blockchains: Ethereum and Ethereum Classic" (Cryptopedia Staff, 2021).

LISTED EXCHANGES
1. How many exchanges is it listed on?
   a. According to etherscan.io, a total of 331 exchanges list Ethereum. That's a lot of options for buying ETH.
2. How easy is it for capital to find it?
   a. The Enterprise Ethereum Alliance (EEA) is a group of over two hundred organizations that adopt and use Ethereum technology in their daily business operations ("Enterprise Ethereum Alliance," 2021).
3. Can you easily exchange your crypto for something else?
   a. Yes, very easily. There are thousands of DApps that are built within the Ethereum ecosystem enabling you to exchange ETH for something else. The hundreds of exchanges that accept ETH also list Bitcoin.

In conclusion, I believe Ethereum is a great investment for many reasons. Ethereum 2.0 addresses all the problems of the network by upgrading its consensus protocol from proof of work to proof of stake. Once this transformation is complete, their active community of users and developers will likely grow, leading to more promising investment returns. Vitalik Buterin is another reason I feel confident investing in Ethereum. The key takeaway from this exercise is to do the research necessary to feel confident in your investment. Maybe when you go through this exercise, you will decide for yourself that Ethereum is not a worthwhile investment. Take the information you learn about the cryptocurrencies you research and feel confident that you are an informed investor because you asked the right questions.

FUTURE: PEOPLE

I believe "The Next Gold Rush" isn't just cryptocurrency or blockchain, it's the next evolution of investing that is made possible because of those technologies. People power every aspect of society, which makes them the fundamental investment in every human institution. Not only are people's coins the next gold rush but they will also be the investors of the gold rush.

The stock market is a market of publicly traded companies with entities like banks, investment firms, and brokerages as the primary investors. Retail investors are individuals who invest in the stock market, but they compete on an uneven playing field. The giant investors get information faster, make trades faster (high frequency trading), and make bigger investments than any individual could make. And when these "too big to fail" firms make bad investments, they get bailed out by the government for fear of the domino effect of their bad decisions (Hogue, 2020).

We need a new market that is made for the people, by the people, and invests in the people. Blockchain technology provides the means to create such a powerful market, which would not rely on an intermediary, making it a purely peer-to-peer investing platform. Similar to how people make investing a full-time job, this could create millions of jobs where individual investors find the most promising people to invest in. I believe not allowing institutions like banks to compete in this new market is the key to keeping it as fair a system as possible. So, the CEO of a major bank would have no advantage over an early adopter to this market of people's coins.

LET'S EXAMINE THE POTENTIAL OF INVESTING IN PEOPLE:

1. Starting out as an adult (eighteen years old), your coin's value will be low, since you have not yet accomplished very much.
2. Assuming your goal is to become wealthy and accumulate assets, your first job is a sign that you are on the right track to achieving that goal.
3. With time and effort, you have built a following, and investors are starting to see a track record of achievements, which translates to your coin's value rising.
4. Maybe you start your own business or make good investments with your resources and investors want to support your successful investments, which creates a virtuous cycle.
5. This process repeats throughout your life with new opportunities and more people that want to support you and also benefit from your successes.

6. Life is full of ups and downs, which your coin will also experience. In the long run, your coin will be a tool to help you overcome life's setbacks.

This is a quick example that shows what an investment in a person would look like and how their coin, which is tied to their worth, appreciates in value over time. It is important to remember that not all people are money-motivated and that there will be many ways to track a person's value.

Another way to measure a person's worth is through their impact. We all make an impact on people, animals, and the environment throughout our lives, yet fail to properly measure our collective impact. These people are conscious of their carbon footprint, volunteer regularly, and abstain from eating animal products. Before Challenge Coin, people still made an impact, but our current system didn't value their impact compared to the money-motivated people in our society. Finally, there is a way for everyone to be valued appropriately.

Investing is not only about making a return on investment, it's also about prioritizing what's important to you. I would argue that the people in our lives who have supported us are the best investments one could make. We build tribes and communities around people, yet we can't invest directly in those people. People are not just assets, they're essential elements to every part of society. We should elevate each other because no one person could be successful without the support of the people that came before them.

What would an index fund for people look like? It could be a collection of the top five hundred technology CEOs or all the employees of a company, which is essentially investing in that company. This would be perfect for investing in online communities or networks of people as well. Imagine being able to invest in the developers who created an open-source technology, like the internet. Investing in all the people that make up a country would be a new way to invest in that country's economy as a people index fund. This is just an idea, but the possibilities are endless. Billions of people use the internet every day, and each one of them is a new opportunity that was undervalued before cryptocurrency.

I see the potential in every person I encounter in my daily life. We all have goals and ambitions for a better tomorrow, and if I had a way to buy peoples' coins to help them, I would. It is the best decision I could make because, like most of us, my sphere of influence is limited to the one hundred or so people that I'm closest to. I have intentionally made time for each of those people, which means that they add value to my life in some way. By investing in them, I also benefit because their lives improve, which means that my life improves through them.

This cycle of improvement and betterment is like a high tide raising all boats. It is time to see investing as an opportunity to collaborate with each other instead of competing to be on top. There is plenty of room in the world for each one of us to succeed, so let us invest in ourselves and the people around us. The future of investing in people is a future of collaboration and mutually beneficial success.

CHAPTER 11:

Evolution of Public Offerings

INITIAL PUBLIC OFFERING (IPO)

"Buying IPOs, for the majority of buyers, isn't investing—it's speculating, as many of the shares allocated in the IPO are flipped the first day. If you really like the stock and plan to hold it as a long-term investment, wait a few weeks or months when the frenzy has disappeared and the price has come down, and then buy it."

—GEORGE GAGLIARDI, CERTIFIED FINANCIAL PLANNER

Before explaining what an initial public offering is, let's discuss why it matters. The ability to offer ownership of a company to the public is an exciting financial innovation. Prior to IPOs, a company was limited to raising capital through sales, debt, or offering equity to wealthy investors. The ability to offer shares of the company to the public made it even easier to raise capital in order to grow the business. The creation of IPOs launched the era of capitalism and corporations, which has made life more convenient for millions of people. One simple idea has changed the world, and one could argue that IPOs have led to the acceleration of growth and prosperity for the modern world (The Investopedia Team, 2020).

The first IPO of the modern era dated back to 1602, when the Dutch East India Company (VOC) offered shares of the company to the public in order to raise capital. The VOC was an international trading and shipping company that had diverse offerings, from trading silks and spices to shipbuilding and production of goods. The VOC was formed from many merchants across the Netherlands into one united company (Phelan, 2016). The reason VOC became public was to appease the merchants that feared a united company where they could lose their money. So, the state decided to offer stock to these merchants, which could be sold as a way for them to get their money out at any time. Those stocks could be sold at the stock exchange in Amsterdam, which was the first exchange in the world (Bragg et al., 2016).

An initial public offering (IPO) is the first sale of a stock by a company to the market. An IPO is a tool that allows smaller companies to get access to capital to grow. This access to capital comes at a price, in the form of paying for financial reporting documents, audit fees, investor relations departments, and accounting oversight committees. In order to even begin the process to IPO, a company must find an investment bank or underwriter to evaluate their financials and generate stocks to sell in a stock exchange (Balasubramaniam, 2020). Underwriter fees are often the most expensive part of an IPO and can range from 3.5 percent to 7 percent based on the deal size. According to PwC, the average range of going public costs between \$9.5 and \$13.1 million (Thomson, 2020).

This is what the very involved process of taking a private company public looks like. The planning preparation phase usually takes one to two years, where the business decides whether or not to pursue an IPO. During this phase, companies will get their books in order, in accordance with acceptable accounting standards, and prepare financial disclosures. Also, management must address regulatory requirements, operational effectiveness, risk management, periodic reporting, and investor relations. A public company requires a team of people who are essential in that transition including accountants, investor relations, PR, legal, and more (Hall, 2020).

After that phase is complete, then the company is ready to go public. This is where a company becomes listed in the stock exchange so the general public can begin investing. To start this process, an investment bank will take the risk of underwriting or becoming owners of the shares of the company. As the underwriter, the bank makes an evaluation of the value of the company, which then translates to a price and number of shares. Those shares are then listed on the stock exchange with the goal of having their prices increase when they are bought by investors (PricewaterhouseCoopers, 2021).

Alibaba Group Holding Limited, also known as Alibaba, released its IPO on September 18, 2014, at the New York Stock Exchange (NYSE). Alibaba is a China-based company that has a diverse portfolio of online businesses including e-commerce, cloud computing, mobile media, and entertainment

("BABA," 2021). Alibaba is a direct competitor with technology giants like Google and Amazon, which made it a popular stock to buy. The underwriter, Credit Suisse, evaluated Alibaba at $21.8 billion, which was the highest valued IPO in history. After some days, the underwriter sold even more shares due to its success, bringing the total IPO to $25 billion (Zucchi, 2020).

Looking at the largest IPOs of all-time, only three of them are US-based. They are General Motors (GM) at #4, which raised $20.1 billion; Visa (V) at #6, which raised $17.9 billion; and Facebook (FB) at #9, which raised $16 billion (Zucchi, 2020). The trends are clear that Asian companies are dominating when it comes to raising large amounts of capital through IPOs. According to PwC's 2020 Global Markets Review, "Globally, there were 1,415 IPOs in 2020, raising a total of $331.3bn, representing a significant increase from 2019 in terms of number of transactions and proceeds (2019: 1,040 IPOs raised $199.2bn)." The frequency and amount raised from IPOs has been going up all over the world.

Coinbase is the largest cryptocurrency exchange in the world and was the first cryptocurrency company to IPO in April 2021. The mixing of the traditional financial sector with the cryptocurrency space will hopefully pave the way for more collaboration in the future. Coinbase has a lot of work to do to appease traditional investors who are nervous about the possibility of hacking and other concerns. This means that the Securities and Exchange Commission will regulate Coinbase's activity, which could also add more security for investors who normally would not invest in cryptocurrencies (DeCambre, 2021). With all these caveats, Coinbase reached a valuation over $100 billion, and according to Don Tapscott, executive chairman of the Blockchain Research Institute, it is "the biggest IPO in history" (James, 2021).

INITIAL COIN OFFERING (ICO)

An initial coin offering (ICO) is a new type of funding for smaller companies that want to raise money by offering tokens instead of shares. Compared to an IPO where larger, more established companies offer equity ownership in return for capital, tokens received during an ICO do not translate to ownership equity in the company. Also, since they are unregulated, ICOs are much riskier and should only be pursued if the investor is prepared to lose their entire investment.

SOME OTHER KEY DIFFERENCES BETWEEN AN ICO AND IPO INCLUDE:

- ICOs have no formal regulatory process, like an IPO working with the SEC, so there is less paperwork involved and fewer legal fees.
- ICOs can occur very quickly compared to an IPO because all you need are programmers, a white paper, and access to the internet.
- An ICO is a riskier investment as startups are more likely to fail compared to established businesses, and cryptocurrency is a relatively new industry ("ICO vs IPO: Key Differences," 2021).

According to GreySpark Partners, 50 percent of ICOs made since 2017 have failed to raise funds, and "the ICO market across the past several years, found that as many as 890 token sales did not raise any funds at all. By contrast, according to the report, 743 token sales were able to reach the $1 million mark. Many token projects fail to provide a positive return-on-investment, particularly as time passes. The report utilized data from ICOData.io and ICO-Check.com through August 2018."

The first Initial Coin Offering was invented in 2012 by J. R. Willett, who is the founder of Mastercoin, which later became Omni. Omni (Mastercoin) is a protocol layer on top of Bitcoin that is similar to Ethereum in that it allows software applications to be built on it. The Omni ecosystem is worth over $2 billion and includes projects like MaidSafe and Tether, which is second only to Ethereum in the value of its asset ecosystem (Willett, 2018).

J. R. Willett explains why he invented the ICO at the Seattle Blockchain Conference: "What I really want to do is raise money from my friends on the Bitcoin forum. That was what drove the whole thing. The venture capital world was a barrier to the way I wanted to raise money. I'll go on to the Bitcoin forum, I'll put my address up, my white paper up, and anybody that sends funds to me owns the new coin. And that was just trying to get around a roadblock."

He continues by saying, "That is what I'm so excited about cryptocurrency, have been since 2010, just that this potential of all these barriers that are in our way—think different things you want to do with money or data to decentralization, the distributed ledger—gets around those things. And if you're using cryptocurrency or a blockchain or a token sale, really you ought to have in the back of your mind, how am I getting around a barrier?"

The idea of circumventing roadblocks or barriers with blockchain technology and cryptocurrency has been a central theme in this book. J. R. Willett is a visionary who saw the power of this technology and its ability to overcome hurdles, and he applied it to investing in companies. ICOs are a fantastic invention, and we are still in the early stages of understanding how impactful they are and will be.

So, what do you own when you invest in an ICO? As mentioned earlier, buying a token does not give you ownership in the project or company. You are essentially buying a perk, like in a crowdfunding campaign. The perk can change based on the specific project, but if your goal is to make money from a company's token, then you are hoping that it appreciates in value. A successful project or ICO launch can have favorable returns for investors generally, based on the greater fool's theory. Basically, any security can increase in value as long as someone else is willing to pay for it. The greater fool is the speculator who is the last to hold the security before it loses its value (Hayes, 2021).

In order to invest in a cryptocurrency startup, I think it's valuable to understand how venture capitalists (VCs) invest in startups. Let's say a VC has invested in ten startups with $1 million invested in each one. Generally, a VC firm is looking to multiply their portfolio's value by ten. For this hypothetical, let's say the value of the portfolio is $50 million, which means they're trying to make $500 million. That means that each company would need to make a $50 million return for the firm to reach its goal. However, startups are risky and oftentimes fail for many reasons that even VCs can't predict. Now, five of the startups have failed, so that's $5 million invested that's gone. In order for the VC to reach their goal, they need the five remaining startups to now make $100 million each.

The strategy of venture capital firms is based on the idea that they really only have to make one or two investments that bring their portfolio's value to over ten times its original worth. This means that all the other investments failed to reach the levels a VC requires to make a giant return. Back to the hypothetical: Out of the five startups that received $1 million, three of them are doing so well that they need more capital to grow. Let's say each startup receives $10 million each. Some time has passed, and one of the three startups that received $10 million is ready to IPO. That company is valued at $1.5 billion, of which the VC owns 50 percent. The return on investment for the VC is 6,718 percent! The other investments breakeven, which makes the total portfolio value worth around $745 Million.

That is a simplified explanation for how VCs make such high returns on their investments. They anticipate that not all the risky startups they invest in will be profitable. But they invest more money into the startups that are profitable, which makes up for the losses of the other investments. In order to invest in even riskier crypto startups, it's time to think like a VC and plan for some failure while doubling down on the successes. General diversification may not be the best investment strategy on its own.

So, you're thinking about investing in an ICO, what are some actionable steps you can take to be an informed investor? Daniel Gouldman is the founder and CEO at Ternio, the enterprise blockchain company that developed the Block-Card, which is fundamentally changing the way in which people interact with their money. The BlockCard allows customers to frictionlessly use their cryptocurrencies in their account and connect it to a Visa card. Daniel and his founders came on the *Crypto 101* podcast to talk about ICOs (Gouldman, 2018).

According to Daniel,

> *If you're looking at an ICO, just right from the start, look at their website. Good website. Look at the [founders] and their backgrounds. Do they have LinkedIn profiles? Are they tackling a problem where they have the right background? Yeah. Do they have an organic community? Yeah. Okay, then it's time to get into the meat of it, the technical details. How does it all function together? Ultimately, there will be things that you don't know. You want to know as much as you can and feel really good that if you're going to make a bet on a startup, that you really understand what's happening under the hood.*

Over the years, there have been some clear winners in the ICO space. Let's examine the highest earning ICO to date with the framework recommended by Daniel. In 2018, EOS raised a record-breaking $4 billion through an ICO. EOS is a platform for decentralized applications that is user-friendly, scalable, high-performing, and secure ("EOS (EOS)—ICO

Rating and Details," 2021). It claims to be the next evolution of blockchain by solving all the problems of previous blockchain projects. The main innovation of EOS is faster speeds with millions of transactions processed per second ("EOSIO Blockchain Software & Services," 2021).

EOS does have a good website that explains what they do: eos.io. ICO Bench is a great website that makes it easy to analyze cryptocurrency startups. It lists their founders and gives them a score of 4.7 out of 5 based on the site's algorithm for trustworthiness. After further review, the founders all have impressive experiences in their LinkedIn profiles that align with the problem they want to solve. At the time of this writing, there are over 680 active DApps within EOS, so there is an organic community (Mulders, 2020). Finally, EOS's whitepaper explains the technical details of what's going on under the hood, like its consensus protocol, which is designed for speed.

The cryptocurrency space is constantly changing and improving itself. ICOs were the breakthrough invention, but now there's new iterations on the idea. Decentralized autonomous initial coin offering (DAICO) empowers investors by giving them control over funds and allowing them to vote on issuing a refund. This motivates the development team to not take and run away with the ICO funds that were raised. Equity token offerings (ETO) or security token offerings (STO) are an equity-crowdfunding tool where companies can issue equity on a blockchain, so investors can buy ownership of the company, like an IPO. STO & ETO are the future of this space, which would not be possible without the ICO, which laid the groundwork (Merre, 2019).

INITIAL PUBLIC PERSON OFFERING (IPPO)

The future is full of possibilities, and I foresee a possible future where "offerings" will extend beyond companies and projects. So far, all the concepts we've discussed—IPO, ICO, DAICO, ETO and STO—are all inventions for companies, both large and small, to raise capital in various ways. What if there was a way for people to raise money with cryptocurrency?

An initial public person offering (IPPO) will be a funding mechanism for people to create their own coin and raise money with it. This is not equity or ownership in a person, so it more closely reflects an ICO than it does an IPO. The breakthrough of this invention is that people can track their worth and benefit financially from it without going into any debt or owing their investors anything in return.

So how do investors make a return on an individual's coin? Even though an investor does not own the person after buying their coin, they do own a stake in value created by that person. The more value that person creates, the more the value of their coin increases. Value is a pretty complex thing to measure, so it is up to the individual to inform their investors how to best measure their coin's value. It could range from assets accumulated, impact of volunteerism, followers on social media and many more. The key is that this personal coin is designed to appreciate in value, like a security, but the underlying asset isn't owned by the investor.

Everyone creates value in many ways, but that value currently gets distributed in ways that generally benefit the middlemen. Decentralization at its purest is peer-to-peer without the need of any bank, company, exchange, government, or other intermediary. An individual's coin is capturing the value of that person without those intermediaries taking a cut.

For instance, when someone works for an employer, they are generally not being paid all the value they create for that employer. Unless the company is flat and all the employees have equity in the company, usually the top of the organizational hierarchy receives most of the value that the company creates. That's why CEO compensation has grown 940 percent since 1978 but typical worker compensation has risen only 12 percent during that time (Mishel and Wolfe 2019). Amazon's CEO, Jeff Bezos, is the richest person in the world, yet his employees are struggling to pay their bills, and more than four thousand of them are on food stamps (Bloomberg News 2020). In order to undo some of the value disparities we see in our society, we need to rethink the distribution of value to favor the individual.

What could this look like in reality? Imagine starting a crowdfunding campaign, similar to Indiegogo or Kickstarter. Instead of selling a product or service, or raising money for a specific cause, you are offering investors the opportunity to buy your coin. This process makes you a public persona, similar to celebrities and politicians, where you are held to a higher standard by the general public. Your investors will want regular updates on the actions you take to accomplish your value creation goals. This can be accomplished through social media or a more formal process similar to how a company has annual shareholder meetings.

Since everyone can create their own coin, there will potentially be billions of new investment opportunities. I envision that finding the best person's coin to invest in will be a full-time job, which will be compensated very well. Hedge fund managers get paid to do the same thing today but for stocks. According to a Gallup Poll, only 55 percent of Americans own stocks, so about half of America does not see any financial benefit from a thriving stock market (Ghilarducci, 2020). IPPO creates a market for peoples' coins that everyone can participate in. This new market for the people would actually create more value for everyone, including those on Wall Street, by making it easier to raise funds and have a better quality of life.

The future implications of the initial public person offering are vast and numerous. Everything that involves people will be impacted, so essentially everything. Cryptocurrency is a new industry that is disrupting all current industries, but IPPOs go even further. People as an asset class are a new industry that creates even more industries and transforms old ones for the better.

CHAPTER 12

The Next Gold Rush

———

"People are your most valuable asset. Only
people can be made to appreciate in value."

—STEPHEN COVEY, AUTHOR OF 7 HABITS
OF HIGHLY EFFECTIVE PEOPLE

YOU: THE NEW ASSET CLASS

An asset class is a group of investments that all share similar
characteristics and are subject to the same regulations. There
are three main asset classes: equities (stocks), fixed income
(bonds), and cash equivalent (USD). Cryptocurrencies are
an emerging asset class that fall into the alternative asset
class segment. There's still debate as to whether or not cryptocurrencies are an asset class. Every asset class is supposed
to have different risk and return investment attributes, and
they perform independently of any given market condition
(Ganti 2021).

In her book, *Cryptocurrencies as an Asset Class? An Empirical Assessment*, Daniele Bianchi concludes, This research, which studies the returns and market activity of the top three hundred cryptocurrencies, shows that, except for a mild correlation with the returns on precious metals, there is no significant relationship between returns on cryptocurrencies and global proxies of traditional asset classes. The absence of cross-assets correlation holds true for both returns and volatility, with the latter indicating that there are no significant spill-over effects in terms of risk between cryptos and more traditional investments.

Essentially cryptocurrencies are a unique asset class compared to more established ones like stocks and bonds. Assuming this remains true into the future, I suspect that there will be even more sub-asset classes within cryptocurrency because of how wide-ranging it can be.

Jake Ryan is the founder and CIO of Tradecraft Capital and author of *Crypto Asset Investing in the Age of Autonomy*. Jake suggests, "I think of the crypto asset class superset a little differently. I would classify the mutually-exclusive subsets based on logical groupings. I see eight distinct crypto asset classes—reserve, currencies, platforms, utility tokens, security tokens, commodities, appcoins, and stablecoins."

Jake further explains, "I use these crypto asset classes because members of the set have similar properties. They have similar functional goals and react to the market in a similar fashion. They have similar valuation models, compete with one another in some form or operate similarly within their set, have similar regulatory risk and generally define the highest subset under the umbrella crypto asset superset."

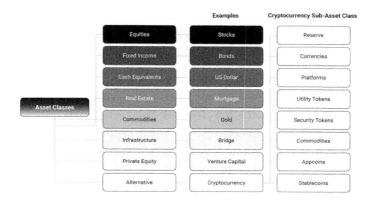

Asset Classes Chart

Cryptocurrency sub-asset classes are important for identifying and categorizing all the various types of cryptocurrencies that exist. At the time of this writing, there are over six thousand seven hundred different cryptocurrencies with multiple functions and use cases. Understanding where each one belongs in the cryptocurrency sub-asset class will help you become a better investor and enthusiast (Royal and Voigt, 2021).

Reserve asset cryptocurrencies are Bitcoin and Ethereum because they are the primary currencies within the cryptocurrency space. When investors need to exchange fiat money for cryptocurrency, they'll usually buy Bitcoin because it's the dominant crypto asset. Ethereum is a close second in that most cryptocurrencies are built within its platform, which gives it special properties for investment purposes.

Currencies are the crypto asset class that primarily function as a payment or medium of exchange. These are most similar to the Cash Equivalents from our list of traditional asset classes. Bitcoin, Bitcoin Cash, Monero, and Dash are examples of cryptocurrencies that are actively trying to let you make payments directly with their coins, like buying coffee at your local coffee shop. These cryptocurrencies all focus on making money faster and more readily available.

Platforms are designed for more cryptocurrencies to be built on top of them. Smart contracts are the primary technology currently used for the creation of decentralized applications. Platforms that allow for smart contracts to be used within them are designated differently because their growth is based on network effects. Some examples of cryptocurrency platforms are EOS, NEO, Cardano, and IOTA.

Utility tokens are cryptocurrencies that are focused on a specific need or utility. Their services are built on top of a platform, usually Ethereum, but in the future may be built on multiple platforms. The value of a utility token comes from network effects and the supply and demand of the tokens. These are examples of some wide-ranging utility tokens: Basic Attention Token (BAT), Civic, and Plensy.

Security tokens are cryptocurrencies whose value is connected to an external asset like a car or a stock. These tokens are a very promising development in the cryptocurrency space, which allows real-life securities to be transacted on the blockchain, similar to the traditional Equities asset class. An example of a security token is Blockchain Capital (BCAP), which was the first tokenized venture fund (Tardif, 2021).

Commodities, within cryptocurrency, are a consumable resource like computing power and storage space. These cryptocurrencies are meant to offer some valuable product or service in return for the token. Crypto-commodities' prices are based on supply and demand of the scarce resource they represent. Here are some examples of commodities: STORJ, FileCoin, and Golem.

Appcoins, or Decentralized Applications (DApps), are the most versatile because they can provide many services. They are usually built on top of a platform and provide applications that are specific to its ecosystem. Some instances of appcoins include Steem, Binance, and SALT.

Stablecoins' core purpose is to provide a stable store of value. Tether is the most popular stablecoin, and it is tied to the value of the US dollar. So, while volatility impacts most cryptocurrencies, stablecoins stay at the price of the asset they're tethered to. Some other stablecoins are Maker, Basecoin, and Digix (Ryan, 2018).

People are the new asset class. Behind the value of every asset is a person who is willing to pay for it. People are the core asset that make cryptocurrency possible. If it wasn't for Satoshi Nakamoto, there would be no Bitcoin; and if Vitalik Buterin never learned about Bitcoin, then he would not have created Ethereum. All these people and the value they create is, simply put, not captured. Why can't I invest in these brilliant entrepreneurs instead of just their businesses?

All people are valuable. There's value in each of us, from our economic output to the relationships we cultivate. Actions like volunteerism and innovation are not properly measured and evaluated based on the people behind their value creation. When you start to see all people as inherently valuable, a switch goes off in your mind, and you can finally appreciate each person as the asset they are.

This isn't to say that we must extract value out of people like a miner who struck gold. It means that we can start to shift our mindsets away from a competitive zero-sum game to get to the top. We should instead think about the collective good we can create by collaborating with one another. Putting a price on the value a person creates will capture the imagination of society. We will finally have more than money as the benchmark for success—we will have self-determined success metrics and overall value contribution as the benchmark.

The next sections will outline two connected roadmaps with how to make this vision a reality. The first roadmap includes actionable steps you can take to continue your crypto journey. The second is a more theoretical roadmap of ideal steps that I plan to take as part of my vision for the future.

ROADMAP TO THE NEXT GOLD RUSH
When I started writing *The Next Gold Rush*, I created a document to reverse engineer my book by starting with the end in mind. Planning for the future often means creating a

roadmap of steps to take in order to get to your end goal. In this section, we'll discuss how you fit into this roadmap with actions that you can take to help further your knowledge and involvement in the cryptocurrency space. Even though this roadmap has instructions on investing, proceed with caution and at your own risk.

ROADMAP:

1. Read this book.
2. Continue your education in cryptocurrency and blockchain.
3. Join cryptocurrency communities, including this reader community.
4. Follow influential cryptocurrency leaders on social media.
5. Buy Bitcoin and store your BTC in a wallet (preferably a cold wallet).
6. Invest in platforms that are building the blockchain infrastructure.
7. Invest in cryptocurrencies that are building the future.
8. Share knowledge about cryptocurrency and blockchain to your connections.
9. Join and invite people to participate in this space.

---

1. READ THIS BOOK.

Congrats! If you are reading this, then you have already accomplished the first step in becoming an educated cryptocurrency enthusiast. You have learned about the importance of cryptocurrency and blockchain technology and the impact it will have on the future.

You are also now a part of a community of people who see value in other people. You can have more discussions with fellow readers about this idea while you continue with your crypto journey.

2. CONTINUE YOUR EDUCATION IN CRYPTOCURRENCY AND BLOCKCHAIN TECHNOLOGY.

Even though I wish you could learn everything there is to know about this topic in my book, the truth is that you have only just dipped your toe into the sea of knowledge that's still expanding. By the time you read this, there will be more innovations, new cryptocurrencies, and more breakthroughs because the rate of change in this industry is incredible.

I interviewed Vanessa Grellet, who is the executive director of global partnerships and alliances at ConsenSys. She said, "There's so much information, but you can't avoid spending time learning. We're in the [cryptocurrency] space, and we're constantly learning and playing catch up because there's innovation topping, left, right, and center. So, it's a constant learning curve. And really try to understand the entire spectrum, because it's not just the miners and the traders and the developers. It's everyone mixed up and working together."

Even the cryptocurrency leaders feel like they are in a constant state of learning in order to keep up with all the innovation that's going on. It is an exciting time to be in the cryptocurrency space, which is still in the early adopter phase. That means most people still don't know about Bitcoin or other cryptocurrencies. A Harris Poll conducted in early 2021 found, "Most people who have heard of cryptocurrencies don't totally get them: 61 percent of people who had heard of the coins said they had little or no understanding of how they work. Only 14 percent of those familiar with crypto said they understand 'very well' how they work" (Wells, 2021).

Being early to the party has some advantages, like lower prices on certain cryptocurrencies before they eventually skyrocket in price after going mainstream. This dynamic occurred in the internet bubble in the early 2000s, but not all internet companies were a good investment. Education is key to figuring out which companies are the next Amazon and Google versus MySpace and Netscape.

Here are top websites to educate yourself on the most popular cryptocurrencies:

- www.coinbase.com/rewards/: Get rewarded with crypto for learning about crypto.
- www.coinmarketcap.com/: List of all active cryptocurrencies by market cap.
- YouTube Channels CryptoCasey, Coin Bureau, and 99Bitcoins are just a few of many fantastic resources for learning more about cryptocurrencies and blockchain technology.

Here are some general educational resources for understanding blockchain technology on a deeper level:

- www.ethereum.org/en/learn/: The Ethereum website provides a wealth of resources for all Ethereum-related questions.

- Udemy, EdX, and Coursera all have free online "Intro to Bitcoin and Cryptocurrencies" classes.
- Subscribe to these reputable crypto news sites: *Cointelegraph, CoinDesk*, and Paul McNeal's www.thecryptocurator.com/.

I had the pleasure of speaking with Paul McNeal about his process for finding the best cryptocurrency news to share with his audience. He goes through all the crypto-related YouTube videos, podcasts, blog posts, and crypto-publications like *NewsBTC*. If you are looking for a reliable starting point for all your crypto news, then check out The Crypto Curator.

3. JOIN CRYPTOCURRENCY COMMUNITIES, INCLUDING THIS READER COMMUNITY.

Joining communities, both online and in-person, is a great way to meet like-minded people. Being able to discuss the concepts you have learned in this book with other people will cement those ideas even more. Also, the added benefit of meeting other interesting people and finding out what motivated them to pursue cryptocurrencies will open discussion about even more topics and idea rabbit holes.

The power of community and tribalism has existed since the beginning of humankind. I personally belong to hundreds of communities from my personal and professional experiences, beliefs, hobbies, activities, and interests. The communities I have joined and people that I've met help define who I am. The cryptocurrency community is full of truth seekers, contrarian thinkers, entrepreneurs, futurists, visionaries, and so many more kinds of people.

You are now part of a tribe of people who see the world differently. We believe in the power of people through decentralization and the power of the peer-to-peer network to change the world for the better. Bitcoin is changing how we think about money and blockchain technology is changing how we think about systems. Systems like the government, banks, corporations, and all central entities can be reimagined with the power of blockchain.

I encourage you to join a cryptocurrency community and start exploring this space and connecting with the people who are in it. You can begin by joining the community of people who have read this book. I will always be available to you as a resource, and the best way to connect with me is through *The Next Gold Rush* reader community on Facebook and Discord. This is a fantastic opportunity to ask questions, meet like-minded people, and stay up to date on the latest developments regarding Challenge Coin.

In addition, here are other thriving cryptocurrency communities you should check out:

- Online:
  - Reddit: r/Cryptocurrency, r/Bitcoin, r/Ethereum
  - Telegram: *ICO SPEAKS NEWS, DeFi Million, Cointelegraph*
  - Discord: Cryptohub, The Crypto Network, Cracking Crypto

- Facebook: Cryptocurrency Collectors Club, Cryptocurrency Academy
- Bitcointalk.org: The original forum that Satoshi Nakamoto created for Bitcoin

- In-person:
  - Meet-up: CryptoMondays, Search "Bitcoin [Your City]" or "Ethereum [Your City]"
  - Crypto Conferences are happening across the globe, all the time.

4. FOLLOW INFLUENTIAL CRYPTOCURRENCY LEADERS ON SOCIAL MEDIA.

Influencers, thought leaders, entrepreneurs, evangelists, and all other kinds of influential cryptocurrency leaders want their followers to learn about cryptocurrency and be informed about developments like current events. Some people have been standing on their soapboxes talking about Bitcoin since its inception in 2009. These are the true believers who understand the mission behind the technology and continue to advocate for its adoption.

I follow many cryptocurrency leaders on different platforms. In my experience, Twitter has the most vocal leaders, but it is the internet, so everywhere you look, you'll find people talking about anything and everything you can imagine. A good place to start is *Cointelegraph's* Top 100 People in Crypto and Blockchain. They update the list of influential people in the cryptocurrency space every year, so I am confident it'll be relevant when you read this.

Twitter is a popular platform to follow crypto influencers like:

- Vitalik Buterin: Founder of Ethereum @VitalikButerin
- Brian Armstrong: Founder of Coinbase @ brian_armstrong
- Andreas Antonopoulos: Crypto author and podcast host @aantonop
- Changpeng Zhao: CEO at Binance: @cz_binance
- Anthony Pompliano: *The Pomp Podcast* host @ APompliano
- Michael Saylor: Founder and CEO at MicroStrategy @ michael_saylor
- Tyler and Cameron Winklevoss: Founders of Gemini @ tyler @cameron
- Don and Alex Tapscott: Founders of Blockchain Research Institute @dtapscott @alextapscott
- Tim Draper: Founder at Draper Associates, DFJ, and Draper University @timdraper

5. BUY BITCOIN AND STORE YOUR BTC IN A WALLET (PREFERABLY A COLD WALLET).

This is an important first step and milestone for all cryptocurrency enthusiasts. Bitcoin is the most widely available and traded cryptocurrency, so if you are not sure where to start then here's a quick breakdown.

You don't need to buy one whole Bitcoin, which is trading around $50,000 at the time of this writing. Let's say you want to invest $100 into Bitcoin. You will actually be buying a fraction of a Bitcoin, which is divided into one hundred million Satoshis. So, $100 at $50,000/BTC buys you two hundred thousand Satoshis. Go to https://coinguides.org/

satoshi-usd-converter/ to find the real-time value of Satoshis compared to the US dollar.

There are a number of ways to buy Bitcoin. The easiest is to go through a popular exchange like Coinbase. Create an account, verify your identity, and then add a payment method. Once all that is done, you should be able to buy Bitcoin and other cryptocurrencies directly on the website.

You should not store your cryptocurrency through exchanges because they are susceptible to getting hacked. That means you could lose all your cryptocurrency if you are not careful. Having a digital wallet is a more secure option for storing your cryptocurrencies. Hot wallets are online and connected to the internet, which means hackers could get access to your private keys. A cold wallet is the safest option for storing your private keys and protecting your cryptocurrency from being stolen.

Hot wallet examples include MetaMask, Mycelium, Electrum, Exodus, CryptX Wallet, and many more.

Trezor and Ledger are the top two manufacturers of cold wallets and offer many different models to choose from.

6. INVEST IN PLATFORMS THAT ARE BUILDING THE BLOCKCHAIN INFRASTRUCTURE.

Ethereum is a platform for decentralized applications, which makes it easier for more cryptocurrency use cases to be created. We need to invest in platforms that are building the infrastructure necessary to continue expanding this space.

I see this investment as being similar to supporting companies that built the internet. Internet service providers (ISPs) like Verizon, AT&T, and Sprint (just to name a few) are responsible for creating the infrastructure and backbone of the internet. Without the success of ISPs, we would not have the internet speeds and availability that we do today (Strickland, 2008).

Some other platforms and important cryptocurrency infrastructure investments include: Cardano, Tezos, Chainlink, Polkadot, Tron, EOSIO, and Cosmos. This isn't a definitive list, but these cryptocurrencies all share common characteristics. They either focus on interoperability, which acts as a bridge between blockchains, or they are platforms that allow other DApps to be built within them.

7. INVEST IN CRYPTOCURRENCIES THAT ARE BUILDING THE FUTURE.

In addition to investing into infrastructure and platforms, we need to also invest in the cryptocurrencies that are making change happen. There are so many applications that are already making big moves to helping people through cryptocurrency.

Challenge Coin is not yet a reality, and until it is, I implore you to find other worthy cryptocurrencies and invest in them. There are plenty of opportunities out there, and if you're having trouble finding them, then follow steps three and four. People are constantly promoting their preferred cryptos to anyone who will listen, so listen.

According to Luke Conway, cryptocurrency expert and associate editor at *Investopedia*, these are "The 10 Most Important Cryptocurrencies Other than Bitcoin":

1. Ethereum (ETH)
2. Litecoin (LTC)
3. Cardano (ADA)
4. Polkadot (DOT)
5. Bitcoin Cash (BCH)
6. Stellar (XLM)
7. Chainlink (LINK)
8. Binance Coin (BNB)
9. Tether (USDT)
10. Monero (XMR)

Note: These are subjective recommendations of literally thousands of cryptocurrencies. Please do your own research and do not invest solely based on what I have written in this book.

8. SHARE YOUR KNOWLEDGE ABOUT CRYPTOCURRENCY WITH YOUR CONNECTIONS.

Just like how avid crypto supporters share their favorite cryptocurrencies in their communities, you need to also become a cryptocurrency advocate. Until the general population is aware of cryptocurrencies and the power it has to improve their lives, we will not see the changes we need. By talking to your friends, family, and followers about cryptocurrency, you are doing your part to educate people about this growing industry.

Network effects are constantly impacting the reach of internet companies and systems. Facebook became the tech giant it is today from network effects, where people share the platform with their friends, who share it with their friends. Virality and shareability are important features of the internet era, but they are also tools that we can use to quickly spread information at scale.

After reading this book and following all the steps up to this point, I hope you believe in the mission and vision of cryptocurrency enough to share it with your connections. After publishing this book, I will probably be talking about cryptocurrencies until the day I die. I'm okay with that because I believe that I'm helping build a movement that's improving the world.

9. JOIN AND INVITE PEOPLE TO PARTICIPATE IN THIS SPACE.

Talking to people and sharing your knowledge with your connections is great work. This step is a continuation of that, but with more follow through. Now that you are having meaningful discussions with your friends, you should help them with their crypto discovery journeys. Invite them to be part of the communities you are in and get them to participate so they too can embrace cryptocurrencies.

Maybe write a book and convince all your friends to buy it so they end up supporting cryptocurrencies and cultivating conversations that you would not otherwise have had with them. If writing a book is too much work (because it really is a lot of work), then start posting about Bitcoin and other cryptocurrencies on your social media. Social media is a fantastic tool to engage your followers at scale. You are essentially updating your entire network at the click of a button.

MY VISION FOR THE FUTURE OF INVESTING IN PEOPLE

From this point on in the roadmap, I'm speaking hypothetically about the future. These future steps outline what I envision happening after publishing this book. I hope you will follow the roadmap as much as possible, which will hopefully lead to the realization of these goals.

ROADMAP CONTINUED:

10. Challenge Coin is created.
11. Create your own coin.
12. Promote your coin on social media and raise funds.
13. Invest in other people's coins to build the community.
14. Continue to be active in the crypto space throughout the adoption process.
15. Normal people are now creating their own coins.
16. Cryptocurrency and blockchain becomes synonymous with the internet.
17. Governments and the establishment change to the will of the people.
18. Challenge Coin becomes the global reserve currency.
19. All people around the world unite under an equitable global economy that doesn't rely on central governments, banks, or corporations.
20. People continue to change the world for the better.
21. The future is here.

---

10. CHALLENGE COIN IS CREATED

This has been a dream of mine for some years now. Challenge Coin will be the cryptocurrency that makes it possible to invest in people by giving people the ability to create their own coins. Another goal of mine is to start the Challenge Company with the mission of overcoming humanity's biggest challenges to make a positive impact on the world. These are big dreams, but the first step toward accomplishing them is writing this book. Then, I can use this book to cultivate a community around this idea, which will hopefully lead to finding passionate people who want to be a part of this journey with me.

I have pitched this idea of people having their own personal coin or currency to practically anyone that would listen and wasn't making progress on building the actual idea. There is a saying in the entrepreneurship world that ideas are worthless by themselves; you need to execute them for them to be valuable. Writing this book is part of my continued attempts to bring this idea to fruition. I am not a developer, and my goal in writing this book is to introduce this idea to technically minded people. Together, we can make Challenge Coin a world-changing reality.

We all benefit from Challenge Coin becoming a reality because we are creating value that did not exist before. We are not taking away from the stock market by creating a market of people's coins. The pie becomes larger when everyone can participate in value creation and when people become a valued asset.

I am not an oracle who can see into the future. I'm just a person with an idea who is determined to make it a reality. This could take a decade or longer to implement, but it will be worth it. This book is the roadmap to creating Challenge

Coin because it will take an entire community to make this idea a reality.

11. CREATE YOUR OWN COIN.

Challenge Coin is now a reality, and you get to be a part of the future people-powered economy. Every person has inherent value, and this is the first cryptocurrency that capitalizes on this idea. By creating your own coin, you are participating in an ecosystem that empowers the people who contribute to it. Whatever your goals are—wealth accumulation, impact, influence, power, etc.—you control your worth.

12. PROMOTE YOUR COIN ON SOCIAL MEDIA AND RAISE FUNDS.

One of the game-changing features of having your own coin is that it captures the value back from social media companies. You can now promote your coin to capture the value of the relationship with your followers. Your coin becomes an extension of your digital identity, so it makes sense that you would promote it everywhere that you have a public profile.

The added benefit is that your online activity becomes a personal crowdfunding campaign where people who want to support you will invest in your coin. You are already seeing this behavior take place with specific campaigns for unexpected financial emergencies and other worthy causes. I suspect that this coin will become the primary tool for raising funds for individuals in the future. Other crowdfunding campaigns will exist, but so far none of them offer a financial benefit to the supporter because they are mainly donation-based.

In effect, everyone is an influencer. Even if you only have a small online following, you still have an influence on those people. Social media has already proved this in the customized feeds and stories we see from people that we follow, large and small. Being able to capture the value that is created from the influencer and follower relationship, in a mutually beneficial way, is a game changer.

Creating your own coin is the first step, but going public is the next step, which requires more obligation and accountability. An initial public person offering (IPPO) is an exciting and momentous milestone for someone as their coin is now considered an asset in which the public can invest. The intrinsic value of that coin comes from the person that created it. Not everyone will go public, but everyone can create their own coin and participate in the people's economy.

13. INVEST IN OTHER PEOPLE'S COINS TO BUILD THE COMMUNITY.

The alternative to going public is to remain private, which means the coin is not available for the general public to invest in. There's still tremendous value to be captured through investing in other people's public coins. Back to the crowdfunding analogy, not everyone creates a campaign, but anyone can invest in a campaign. The same applies to people's coins.

14. CONTINUE TO BE ACTIVE IN THE CRYPTO SPACE THROUGHOUT THE ADOPTION PROCESS.

Fast forward to a thriving economy of people creating their own coins and investing in other people's coins. This new marketplace of the people, for the people, and by the people is continuing to grow because of people like you who actively advocate for it.

With any human institution or system that was invented by people like the government, money, corporations, laws, etc., we all need to collectively agree and believe in the idea for it to be real. Cryptocurrency is no exception. Bitcoin would have no value if no one ever bought it or believed it could act as a store of value. Satoshi Nakamoto planted the seeds of Bitcoin but the people that believed in the idea of Bitcoin and its future potential are the ones who made it valuable.

The best ideas are the ones that stand the test of time. Democracy, for instance, has weathered many storms, from wars to authoritarianism. Certain technologies like fax machines and VCRs do not survive the test of time. Only time will tell which ideas and innovations will become the future and which will remain a part of the past.

Assuming Challenge Coin is an idea that will be a part of the future, I envision that the natural behavior of sharing your coin in your networks will, relatively quickly, spread across the internet and around the world. In that sense, the goal of mass adoption is like a self-fulfilling prophecy because network effects are built into the idea.

15. NORMAL PEOPLE ARE NOW CREATING THEIR OWN COINS.

The normal people I am referring to are the mainstream, or late majority, of the adoption curve. At this point, hundreds of millions of people have created their own coins and are actively promoting them online. It can be hard to imagine, so let me paint a picture for you.

The internet today is all about attention and consumerism. Every company, for the most part, is vying for your eyeballs or your money. With Challenge Coin, there is an option that focuses on people and their success. It flips the script from companies benefiting from your attention and consumerism to people getting the opportunity to capitalize on their own relationships and value creation.

16. CRYPTOCURRENCY AND BLOCKCHAIN BECOMES SYNONYMOUS WITH THE INTERNET.

When Challenge Coin becomes mainstream, it will reach its greatest power and influence. At that point, I imagine that cryptocurrency and blockchain will become synonymous with the internet. My reasoning is that Bitcoin will also gain traction over time; it has had a head start since its inception in 2009.

The success of one cryptocurrency is a success for all cryptocurrencies. That is basically why the price of Bitcoin is connected to the prices of all other cryptocurrencies. When the price of Bitcoin skyrockets, the prices of other cryptocurrencies increase as well.

17. GOVERNMENTS AND THE ESTABLISHMENT CHANGE TO THE WILL OF THE PEOPLE.

I foresee that the more mainstream cryptocurrency becomes, the more the establishment has to change. Cryptocurrencies are the key to the largest redistribution of power to normal people since Franklin Delano Roosevelt's New Deal. There's probably going to be a big battle before this happens, but the government is out of touch with the people it's supposed to represent, and ultimately that will lead to its downfall, possibly via the next big bubble.

Blockchain offers many ways to change the government. In a previous chapter, we discussed one scenario where politicians can create a coin to fundraise for their political campaigns. That just scratches the surface of blockchain use cases for politics. Plenty of other processes would benefit from blockchain, like voting, transparency, accountability, self-governing, and more which will become a reality with the rise of cryptocurrency.

18. CHALLENGE COIN BECOMES THE GLOBAL RESERVE CURRENCY.

What is a global reserve currency? In 1944, the US dollar officially became the world's reserve currency, following the Bretton Woods Agreement (Chen, 2020). The currency of tomorrow will be independent of governments and central banks, so the definition of a global reserve currency will likely change. Right now, Bitcoin has the best chance of being the next global currency, but I don't believe it will remain that way.

Challenge Coin is a collection of all peoples' coins, and if you extrapolate that out to the global population, then you essentially have a cryptocurrency that represents the entire world. Not even Bitcoin can claim to potentially represent the entire population, mainly because there is a limit on the amount of Bitcoins that will ever be created, twenty-one million. And what we are already seeing is that primarily, the rich are buying most of the available Bitcoins. The distribution of wealth in Bitcoin is still unbalanced with whales, institutional investors, miners, and a handful of early adopters owning most Bitcoins available.

The limit of the amount of Challenge Coins is dependent on the population and the number of people who create their own currencies. Each individual's currency is part of an ecosystem that can make up everyone. Governments' currencies represent the people within them, so this would be like creating a United Nations currency that represented all governments and their citizens.

19. ALL PEOPLE AROUND THE WORLD UNITE UNDER AN EQUITABLE GLOBAL ECONOMY THAT DOESN'T RELY ON CENTRAL GOVERNMENTS, BANKS, OR CORPORATIONS.

No one can predict the future, myself included. I am merely prophesying for the sake of discussing a best-case scenario worth achieving. If I'm off and the future isn't as great as I am predicting, well, I'm content with shooting for the stars and reaching the moon. Let's collectively agree that this is a moonshot worth pursuing and suspend judgement until we do what's in our power to make our future a reality.

The power of central governments, banks, and corporations has reached historic levels. The internet has made these entities even more powerful, but cryptocurrency and blockchain technology could eventually make them obsolete. All the gatekeepers, status quo managers, and intermediaries are in for a rude awakening because the power is going to come back to the people.

20. PEOPLE CONTINUE TO CHANGE THE WORLD FOR THE BETTER.

If the past is any indication of the future, then I'm cautiously optimistic. We have had some close calls as a species, but we've persevered and evolved. There are unprecedented global threats that we need to address like climate change, overpopulation, wealth inequality, and more. These challenges are not impossible to overcome because nothing is impossible when we work together. Blockchain is a return to the internet's decentralized beginnings, which was a focus on connecting people from all over the world.

21. THE FUTURE IS HERE.

Everyone has a picture in their head. They have a goal or some future possibility that motivates them. The future is unknown, yet we all believe in our own visions of the future.

I believe in a future that some people say is unrealistic. It may be improbable, but I believe it is possible, nonetheless. Some may say it is too utopian. Some may say it is naive. These people need to dream bigger and not limit the dreams of others.

Visions, dreams, and future goals are all just things we imagine, so why not imagine the best, most brilliant thing imaginable?

I have a vision of the future where people work together around the world. We work together to solve the biggest problems humanity has ever faced. Solving problems is not inherently unrealistic, but cooperation at a global scale has been. Blockchain technology and cryptocurrencies can change that.

We are so divided in so many ways that we can't see the power of cooperation. Capitalistic competition has blinded us to the exponential rewards of collaboration. Why is it so hard to put aside our differences for the common good?

It is in our best interest to work together, so let us be the change we want to see in the world. The first step is sometimes the hardest, but in this case, it is easy. I want you to dream of the best future you can imagine.

Then ask yourself, can I make this dream a reality today? Is there some small thing I can do that inches me closer to that future possibility?

Even if the dream is not realized completely, the world will have been better for the small changes you made to bring the future closer to the present.

CONCLUSION

TL;DR

TOO LONG; DIDN'T READ

This book has been divided into three sections for three groups of people: Crypto-Curious, Crypto-Conscious, and Crypto-Capitalist. Crypto-Curious people are curious about cryptocurrency and want to learn more. Crypto-Conscious people already know some of the basics of cryptocurrency but are intrigued about how it might become more relevant and accessible to their lives. Crypto-Capitalists are more advanced people who are looking for investment advice or future cryptocurrency ideas that have the potential to make it big.

The first section, for the Crypto-Curious, discussed the basics of cryptocurrency and blockchain. Then, we talked about what Bitcoin and Ethereum are and learned about their founders. Debt and credit systems are human systems that have been quintessential in the development of money. Cryptocurrency is the digital evolution of money, and it builds on the ideas of credit systems with the power of technological accountability. Bubbles reoccur throughout history because of human behavior and will likely keep happening far into the future. Lastly, I introduced my idea for Challenge Coin and discussed how people will be able to create their own personal currency in the future.

The second section, for the Crypto-Conscious, explores use cases for how cryptocurrency will impact different industries. Politics is generally slow to evolve, but that could change once politicians fundraise their campaigns through cryptocurrency. Entrepreneurs require capital for their startups, which are considered high-risk investments that often fail. If an entrepreneur raises capital by creating their own coin, then even if the startup fails, the entrepreneur continues, which decreases the risk for the investor. The influencer and follower relationship will also change with cryptocurrency, becoming a direct relationship where both parties can benefit financially. Then, we explore the life cycle of your coin and what it might look like to create a coin and use it to raise money throughout your life.

The last section, for the Crypto-Capitalists, is about investing in cryptocurrency while understanding the risks of doing so. I laid out the common scams, hacks, cons, and other things to look out for before investing in cryptocurrency. The investing fundamentals are important as well, so I explained short-term versus long-term investing strategies and showcased the cryptocurrency evaluation tool. The evolution of public offerings demonstrates the trend of companies getting access to capital and how people will be able to raise capital similarly with cryptocurrency. Finally, the concept of people as a new asset class is explained in detail alongside a roadmap of how to make this idea a reality.

MY VISION FOR THE FUTURE

Let's jump in my time machine into the not-too-distant future. This is the future I want to live in and one in which, hopefully, you will too.

My name is Ethan Turer, and I'm the CEO of the Challenge Company. We tackle some of the world's biggest challenges, like world hunger and wealth inequality. The first challenge we worked on was fixing the inequities of our global economy. More specifically, the people that were already rich in our society kept getting richer while the poor and middle class were left to survive on the trickling-down of wealth from those at the top. This system was unsustainable and immoral, so the brilliant minds at the Challenge Company created a new system that is designed to work for everyone, not just the wealthy and elites. Now, people can have a level playing field while they are trying to work their way to the top instead of a rigged game designed to maintain the status quo.

This new human system paved the way for a generation of creators to flourish with the ability to build communities and capitalize on their influencer/follower relationship more effectively. Musicians, artists, authors, entrepreneurs, and any other influencer you can think of all benefited from this new economic system. However, the real beneficiaries were the followers; because for the first time, people could invest in other people. Influencers used to sell merchandise, create sponsored content, and gain subscribers on sites, like Patreon, to make a living. By investing in the influencer's coin, then your investment appreciates over time, based on the growth of the influencer's community and brand. So now, both influencers and followers can be rewarded for doing the same community building activities that they are already doing in the internet era.

Politicians are supposed to represent the people that vote them into office. In the future, I want to live in a world where that's exactly what they'll do. Our current problem is that politicians accept donations from special interest groups and wealthy donors in order to get elected. Thus, the voices of those donors overshadow the needs of their constituents. If every politician created a coin to fund their political campaigns, then all the donations would be publicly funded. The best part is that the voters who buy that politician's coin can sell it as well. This completely changes the feedback loop in our current system, where voters donate a certain amount and then have no other means of having their voices heard, besides voting. Imagine Politician X runs on a campaign of transparency to the public and then news breaks of some sketchy deal that was made behind closed doors. Well, now all the people who bought Politician X's coin can sell it and let that politician suffer the consequences of their actions.

All this is possible because of an idea I had back in 2018 for a new kind of cryptocurrency. My idea is to create a cryptocurrency that would allow every person to have their own coin connected to their worth. Currently, the richest people are evaluated by *Forbes* in their "top richest people in the world" segment, based on the assets they have accumulated. What about the rest of us? Do we want to compare each other based on accumulation of wealth? If we had a different method to evaluate people other than money, wealth, profits, and capital gains, then we are one step closer to living in a better world.

Let's use me as an example. I am an early-stage entrepreneur with little to no assets and no previous experience running a company. It would be very hard, almost impossible, to find an investor who would invest in my first startup, which statistically is likely to fail. If I instead created Ethan Coin and asked investors to buy my coin to fund the startup, then even if the first startup fails, Ethan Coin isn't a failure, because those same investors would already be invested in the next company I start via Ethan Coin. Even if I don't create another company, I will still find ways to improve my quality of life over time, and that's how Ethan Coin measures value—not just monetary quality, but also through metrics like hours volunteered, number of followers, health, and so much more.

So, it's less risky for investors because people generally bounce back over the course of their lives. The other interesting aspect of this idea is that I'm creating a new asset class, so people would become tradeable, like trading stocks in the stock market. Except instead of companies, you're trading people's coins. If you think about it, what are companies except a collection of people? There are endless possibilities for how people creating their own personal currency can change society for the better, and I am excited to make this idea a reality.

The new economic system is limitless, since every person can create their own coin, which means that everyone may have their own mission for raising funds. The next gold rush is in cryptocurrency, but it is not investing in Bitcoin, it's investing in people. People are the backbone of society and human institutions. We make up every community, company, government, institution, and country. Collectively, people are the global economy and have the power to shape the world. So, creating a new economic system is no small feat, but it is an essential change that can lead to changing how we do everything.

HOW DO WE MAKE THIS IDEA A REALITY?

There are certain steps that need to happen before Challenge Coin is created. The first step is reading this book. Congrats on completing the first step! Your education does not end here, though; you should continue your education and learn more about cryptocurrency and blockchain. Join cryptocurrency communities, including this reader community. Learn from others who are like-minded, which will help you stay up to date on the latest developments in this space. Follow influential cryptocurrency leaders on social media to learn from the people who are leading the change and have a bird's eye view of the industry.

Once you feel comfortable enough, I recommend learning by doing. So, buy Bitcoin and store your BTC in a wallet, preferably a cold (hardware) wallet. Do not buy more than you can afford to lose, and don't buy so much that you can't sleep at night. Invest in platforms that are building the blockchain infrastructure, which will allow even more innovations to be developed in the future. Invest in cryptocurrencies that are building the future of tomorrow, today. Remember that it is important to share your knowledge about cryptocurrency and blockchain with your connections. The crypto community can only grow if people like you are willing to share what you know with your friends, family, and followers. Last but not least, join and invite people to participate in this space.

Talking is great, but your impact grows exponentially when others go down the cryptocurrency rabbit hole and start their own crypto journeys.

Even if you decide not to pursue a journey with cryptocurrency beyond reading this book, I want to thank you for your time. Time is our most valuable resource, and if I was able to inspire you or get you thinking about the world in a different way, then I feel that I did my job as an author. Remember that your time is a precious commodity, and cryptocurrency will redistribute the flow of value of your time from the wealthy, powerful, and elites back to the source, you. This fundamental change is what excites me the most about the future of cryptocurrency, and I hope it excites you too.

ACKNOWLEDGEMENTS

This book would not be possible without the love and support of many people in my life. First, I'd like to thank my family: Shellie, Shane, and Nicole. We have been through thick and thin together, including a pandemic. I would not be where I am today without you guys, and I'm forever grateful for everything you've done for me. Love you to the moon and back again.

Thank you to the rest of my family for all your support, especially with my pre-order campaign. I appreciate all my friends who have probably gotten sick of me talking about cryptocurrency over the years but have supported me anyway. Special shout-out to Shellie Prezant, Tim Elkana, John Staver, Joshua Landis, Kendy Land, Elaine Adelman, Dan Weeks, Teri Prezant, Eric Koester, and Hannah Aksamit for supporting my book campaign launch.

A HUGE thank you to my most generous supporters: Lynn Metcalf, Ryan Ross, Joel Greco, Stephen Kaczynski, Giorgi Paikidze, Christi Robinson, Adrian Eaton, Shellie Prezant, and Teri Prezant. There are so many people who supported my book campaign that I am going to acknowledge, but I just want to say that I'm eternally grateful for every one of you.

In 2020, when I was looking for "what's next?" I found out that my friend, Alyssa Mavor, was writing a book called *The Art of the Moonshot*. She introduced me to the program she was using for her author journey, developed by Eric Koester and the Creator Institute, which inspired me pursue my dream and write this book. Sometimes, when you're looking for something, life finds a way to help you find it.

As a first-time author, I could not have completed my manuscript without my editors, Al Bagdonas and Chuck Oexmann. Their dedication to the craft while providing constructive feedback and challenging my ideas turned my manuscript into a book worth reading. I'm so lucky to have had an author community to support me throughout this writing process. Thank you Komal Shah, Sasi Yajamanyam, Ester Teper, and Mohamad Yassin for keeping me accountable and encouraging me to keep going. Komal and I have spent countless hours together on Zoom revising our books together, a motivating rhythm without which I don't know if I could have put in the hours to get this done, so thank you.

Thank you to my beta readers, who read my book early and provided critical feedback for me to make improvements. I owe Adrian Eaton, Kendy Land, Carol Kerwin, and Tim Elkana so much for taking the time to read most, if not all, of my manuscript. All the feedback I've received has been so helpful, so thank you also to Stephen Box, Sebastien Arbogast, Hannah Aksamit, and Christi Robinson.

Many of the ideas in this book have been shaped by the many people I had the pleasure of interviewing. Even if they were not directly cited in the final cut, I'd like to acknowledge their contribution and time spent talking with me. Thank you to Mark Sheldon of John Carroll University, George Gvazava of CryptX Wallet, Brandi Kolosky and Sam Errama of Plensy, John Nance of Deal Box, Sebastien Arbogast of ChainSkills, Joel Comm of Bad Crypto Podcast, Amit Kaushik of Bitcoin Investor, Amber Perkins of Tradehouse Investment Group, Ron Rubine of LA CD12, Alex Barry of Quantify Crypto, and Ben Erwin of Powersimple. I'm especially grateful to the CryptX Wallet team for their continued support. There are many more people who have impacted my writing, so thank you, because writing a book takes a community.

Speaking of community, I'm so grateful to the Cal Poly Entrepreneurs Club, Cal Poly, and the many other communities that have helped me grow into the person I am today. People are what make life worth living, and I'm so lucky to have an amazing network of people who support me and care about me. Thank you everyone, and I hope this book has got you thinking about the value of the people in your life.

Thank you to all the amazing people who pre-ordered my book:

Adrian Eaton, Alex White-Gomez, Alexa Rozell, Alexander Gierczyk, Alyssa Espinola, Alyssa Mavor, Amber Perkins, Andrew Dicken-Prince, Andrew Laron, Andrew Thayer, Angelic Dirden, Anthony Hakim, Ariana Torres, Axel Aguado, Barbara Turbyville, Betty Turer, Blake Zabrek, Bobby Naimark, Bonnie Wolf-Moss, Bradley Splettstoesser, Brenda

Ross, Brian Wickstrom, Carol Kerwin, Carolyn Anhalt, Chad Lagomarsino, Chelsea Brown, Christi Robinson, Christopher McCullough, Craig Anderson, Daniel Wolfe, Dan Weeks, Darryl Giors, Davey Saba, David Rudolph, Debbie Schwartz, Debbie Turer, delizero, Dylan Harari, Elaine Adelman, Eli Burch, Eric Fisher, Eric Koester, Frances Plotkin, George Will, Giorgi Paikidze, Greg Lampel, Gregg N Willcox, Hannah Aksamit, Hans Hustace, Ian Alexander, Ian Rice, Ivy Au, James Schulte, James Young, Jarid Matylewicz, Jasmine Yu, Javier Garcia, Jennifer Anderson, Jessie Franco, Jim Harris, Jim Fenwick, Joe Rosenbaum, Joel Greco, Joey Lyman, John Staver, John Townsend, Jonathan Keene, Jonathan York, Jorge Ehlers, Jose Adan Govea, Josh Cohen, Josh Rehhaut, Joshua Broad, Joshua Landis, Julia Howelman, Julia Switzky, Julian Tabalujan, Kara Paolilli, Karen Tyler, Karina Torres, Kate Newton, Kendy Land, Kyle Hanger, Lars Riemenschneider, Lilian Chen, Lynn Metcalf, Louis Rosenberg, Lucas Bashaar, Lucas Estes, Luke Fox, Maggie Von Stein, Marc Shenton, Mark Calver, Mark Sheldon, Martha Oregel, Martyn Henderson, Matt McGunagle, Matt Ghiglieri, Maureen Ilumin, mcrtweb, Melanie Anderson, Michael Amicarelli, Mitchell Aiken, Morassa Danai, Nathan Vaughan, Nicholas K Thompson, Nick Andre, Nick Aukland, Nicole Turer, Nicole Woo, Omri Nissan, Patrick Huffman, Paul McNeal, Payton Thatcher, Rich Mob Paladino, Rikki Gerald, Ryan Ross, Sam Errama, Sasi Yajamanyam, Sean Reilly, Sebastien Arbogast, Semee Park, Shane Turer, Shel Prezant, Shellie Prezant, Slater McLean, Sophie Richman, Jeffrey Ringer, Stephen Box, Stephen Kaczynski, Sydney Harder, Tania Real, Teri Prezant, Tiffany Pan, Timothy Elkana, Tom Bunting, Toni Prezant, Tushar Shah, Tyler Haaland, Will Armstrong, Zubin Adrianvala

BIBLIOGRAPHY

INTRODUCTION

Board of Governors of the Federal Reserve System. "The Fed—Dealing with Unexpected Expenses." May 28, 2019. https://www.federalreserve.gov/publications/2019-economic-well-being-of-us-households-in-2018-dealing-with-unexpected-expenses.htm.

Dolan, Kerry, ed. 2021. *The Forbes 400*. Forbes, 2021.

Horowitz, Juliana, Ruth Igielnik, and Rakesh Kochhar. "Trends in US Income and Wealth Inequality." Pew Research Center's Social & Demographic Trends Project. January 9, 2020. https://www.pewresearch.org/social-trends/2020/01/09/trends-in-income-and-wealth-inequality/.

Kotashev, Kyril, and Nicolás Cerdeira. "The Ultimate Startup Failure Rate Report [2021]." Failory.com. March 5, 2021. https://www.failory.com/blog/startup-failure-rate.

Oxfam International. "5 Shocking Facts about Extreme Global Inequality and How to Even It up." October 4, 2019. https://www.oxfam.org/en/5-shocking-facts-about-extreme-global-inequality-and-how-even-it.

Thiel, Peter, and Blake Masters. *Zero to One: Notes on Startups, or How to Build the Future.* New York: Crown Business. September 16, 2014.

CHAPTER 1

Buterin, Vitalik. "Ethereum Whitepaper." Ethereum.org. February 9, 2021. https://ethereum.org/en/whitepaper/.

Casey, Crypto. "Ethereum 2021 Explained: What Is Ethereum & How It Works (Ultimate Beginner's Guide)." www.youtube.com. February 29, 2020. Video, 23:46. https://www.youtube.com/watch?v=DhoRtGCp4JI&ab_channel=CryptoCasey.

Chohan, Usman W. "The Double Spending Problem and Cryptocurrencies." Papers.ssrn.com. January 6, 2021. https://papers.ssrn.com/sol3/papers.cfm?abstract_id=3090174.

CoinGecko. "Bitcoin (BTC) Price, Marketcap, Chart, and Info." Accessed on April 20, 2021. https://www.coingecko.com/en/coins/Bitcoin.

Cointelegraph. "Who Is Vitalik Buterin." Accessed on April 20, 2021. https://cointelegraph.com/ethereum-for-beginners/who-is-vitalik-buterin#:~:text=Vitalik%20Buterin%20is%20a%20Russian.

Ethereum.org. "What Is Ethereum?" Accessed on April 20, 2021. https://ethereum.org/en/what-is-ethereum/?.

Feins, William. "Satoshi Nakamoto." Euro Cheddar. August 16, 2017. http://www.eurocheddar.com/profiles-in-europe/ satoshi-nakamoto-creator-Bitcoin/.

Lai, Victor. "Introduction to Cryptography in Blockchain Technology." Crush Crypto. December 19, 2018. https://crushcrypto. com/cryptography-in-blockchain/#:~:text=Cryptography%20 is%20an%20integral%20part.

Lammle, Rob. "A Brief History of Challenge Coins." www.mentalfloss.com. September 26, 2012. https://www.mentalfloss.com/ article/12630/brief-history-challenge-coins.

Land, Kendy. "All about Consensus Protocols, Mining, & Staking." Crypt Keepers. Accessed on April 20, 2021. https://www. cryptkeepers.club/consensus-protocol-academy-glossary.html.

Martin, Nate. "What Is Bitcoin? Bitcoin Explained Simply for Dummies." www.youtube.com. 99Bitcoins. April 4, 2018. Video, 12:48. https://www.youtube.com/watch?v=41JCpzvn-n_0&ab_channel=99Bitcoins99Bitcoins.

Martin, Nate. "What Is Ethereum? A Beginner's Explanation in Plain English." www.youtube.com. June 26, 2018. Video, 11:49. https://www.youtube.com/watch?v=jxLkbJozKbY&t=29s&ab_ channel=99Bitcoins.

Millman, Rene. "What Is Ethereum 2.0 and Why Does It Matter?" Decrypt. December 1, 2020. https://decrypt.co/resources/what-is-ethereum-2-0.

Nakamoto, Satoshi. "Bitcoin: A Peer-To-Peer Electronic Cash System." Bitcoin.org. Accessed on April 20, 2021. https://Bitcoin.org/Bitcoin.pdf.

Nolen, Jeannette. "Emergency Economic Stabilization Act of 2008." In *Encyclopædia Britannica*. Accessed on April 20, 2021. https://www.britannica.com/topic/Emergency-Economic-Stabilization-Act-of-2008.

Oliver, John. "Cryptocurrencies: Last Week Tonight with John Oliver (HBO)." www.youtube.com. March 11, 2018. Video, 25:20. https://www.youtube.com/watch?v=g6iDZspbRMg&t=3s.

Peck, Morgen. "The Uncanny Mind That Built Ethereum." *Wired*. June 13, 2016. https://www.wired.com/2016/06/the-uncanny-mind-that-built-ethereum/.

Phillips, Daniel. "How Many Bitcoin Does Its Inventor Satoshi Nakamoto Still Own?" *Decrypt*. January 3, 2021. https://decrypt.co/34810/how-many-Bitcoin-does-its-inventor-satoshi-nakamoto-still-own.

Rosulek, Martin. "14 Bitcoin Quotes by Famous People." *Medium*. August 24, 2017. https://medium.com/@MartinRosulek/14-Bitcoin-quotes-by-famous-people-6e7a1a009281.

Singh, Manoj. "The 2007–08 Financial Crisis in Review." *Investo-pedia*. July 26, 2020. https://www.investopedia.com/articles/economics/09/financial-crisis-review.asp.

"State of the DApps — DApp Statistics." www.stateofthedapps.com. Accessed on April 20, 2021. https://www.stateofthedapps.com/stats/platform/ethereum.

Yglesias, Matthew. "The Fed and the 2008 Financial Crisis." *Vox*. June 21, 2014. https://www.vox.com/2014/6/20/18079946/fed-vs-crisis.

CHAPTER 2

Ammous, Saifedean. *The Bitcoin Standard: The Decentralized Alternative to Central Banking*. Hoboken, New Jersey: John Wiley & Sons, Inc., 2018.

Coppola, Frances. "Why Bitcoin Thrives (and Why It Won't Replace the Dollar)." *CoinDesk*. November 16, 2020. https://www.coindesk.com/why-Bitcoin-thrives-wont-replace-dollar.

Dickler, Jessica. "Raw Deal: The Incredible Shrinking Cereal Box - Sep. 10, 2008." Money.cnn.com. September 10, 2008. https://money.cnn.com/2008/09/09/pf/food_downsizing/.

Hanyecz, Laszlo. Accessed on April 20, 2021. IMG_0984.Jpg. Http://Heliacal.net/~Solar/Bitcoin/Pizza/.

Hayes, Adam. "What Happens to Bitcoin after All 21 Million Are Mined?" *Investopedia*. February 28, 2021. https://www.

investopedia.com/tech/what-happens-Bitcoin-after-21-million-mined/#:~:text=transactions%20with%20fees.-.

Lewis, Antony. *The Basics of Bitcoins and Blockchains: An Introduction to Cryptocurrencies and the Technology That Powers Them*. Coral Gables: Mango Publishing, 2018.

Lips, Ferdinand. *Gold Wars: The Battle against Sound Money as Seen from a Swiss Perspective*. Fame (Foundation for the Advancement Of), 2001

Maloney, Michael. *Guide to Investing in Gold and Silver: Protect Your Financial Future*. Scottsdale, Arizona: RDA Press, 2008.

Maloney, Mike. "Money vs Currency—Hidden Secrets of Money Episode 1—Mike Maloney." February 26, 2013. Video, 25:55. https://www.youtube.com/watch?v=DyVoO-fU3-FU&list=PLE88E9ICdiphYjJkeeLL2Oo9eJoC8r7Dc&index=1&ab_channel=GoldSilver%28w%2FMikeMaloney%29.

Maloney, Mike. "Fall of Empires: Rome vs USA (Hidden Secrets of Money Ep 9)." October 29, 2018. Video, 28:27. https://www.youtube.com/watch?v=OuOcnGAv4oo&list=PLE88E9ICdiphYjJkeeLL2Oo9eJoC8r7Dc&index=9&ab_channel=GoldSilver%28w%2FMikeMaloney%29.

Merchant, Brian. "This Pizza Cost $750,000." www.vice.com. March 26, 2013. https://www.vice.com/en/article/yppj8b/this-pizza-is-worth-750000.

Moore, Galen. "10 Years On, Laszlo Hanyecz Has No Regrets about His $45M Bitcoin Pizzas." *CoinDesk*. May 22, 2020. https:// www.coindesk.com/Bitcoin-pizza-10-years-laszlo-hanyecz.

Nixon, Richard. "Address to the Nation Outlining a New Economic Policy: 'the Challenge of Peace.'" www.presidency.ucsb. edu. August 15, 1971. https://www.presidency.ucsb.edu/documents/address-the-nation-outlining-new-economic-policy-the-challenge-peace.

Santayana, George. *The Life of Reason: Introduction and Reason in Common Sense*. 1905. https://santayana.iupui.edu/wp-content/ uploads/2019/01/Common-Sense-ebook.pdf.

Team, Goldma. "Currency vs Money: Did You Know There's a Difference?" *Medium*. October 3, 2018. https://medium.com/@ goldma/currency-vs-money-did-you-know-theres-a-difference-f344aa496867.

Tether. "Tether." July 12, 2014. https://Tether.to.

www.inflationtool.com. "Value of 1971 US Dollars Today - Inflation Calculator." Accessed on April 20, 2021. https://www.inflationtool.com/us-dollar/1971-to-present-value.

CHAPTER 3

Coindesk. "Bitcoin Price Index—Real-Time Bitcoin Price Charts." *CoinDesk*. Accessed on April 20, 2021. https://www.coindesk. com/price/Bitcoin.

Board of Governors of the Federal Reserve System. "Federal Reserve Board—Recent Balance Sheet Trends." June 25, 2021. https://www.federalreserve.gov/monetarypolicy/bst_recent-trends.htm.

Gaither, Chris, and Dawn Chmielewski. "Fears of Dot-Com Crash, Version 2.0." *Los Angeles Times*. July 16, 2006. https://www.latimes.com/archives/la-xpm-2006-jul-16-fi-overheat16-story.html.

HistoryNet. "California Gold Rush." Accessed on April 20, 2021. https://www.historynet.com/california-gold-rush.

Kleinbard, David. "Dot.coms Lose $1.755 Trillion in Market Value - Nov. 9, 2000." *CNN*. November 9, 2000. https://money.cnn.com/2000/11/09/technology/overview/.

Lusk, Veneta. "The Market Crash of 2008 Explained." *Wealthsimple*. June 4, 2019. https://www.wealthsimple.com/en-us/learn/2008-market-crash#what_date_in_2008_did_the_stock_market_crash.

Malkiel, Burton G. *Random Walk Down Wall Street: The Time-Tested Strategy for Successful Investing*. W. W. Norton, 1973.

Murphy, Chris. "Assessing a Stock's Future with the Price-To-Earnings Ratio and PEG." *Investopedia*. January 30, 2021. https://www.investopedia.com/investing/use-pe-ratio-and-peg-to-tell-stocks-future/.

Nankin, Jesse, and Krista Schmidt. "History of US Gov't Bailouts." *ProPublica*. April 15, 2009. https://www.propublica.org/article/government-bailouts.

Roberts, Lance. "Technically Speaking: Blowing up the Everything Bubble." Seekingalpha.com. February 23, 2021. https://seekingalpha.com/article/4408272-technically-speaking-blowing-up-the-everything-bubble.

Whitbourne, Kathryn, and Francisco Guzman. "How Much Actual Money Is There in the World?" *HowStuffWorks*. May 21, 2021. https://money.howstuffworks.com/how-much-money-is-in-the-world.htm.

CHAPTER 4

Benfer, Emily, David Robinson, Stacy Butler, Lavar Edmonds, Sam Gilman, Katherine McKay, Zach Neumann, Lisa Owens, Niel Steinkamp, and Diane Yentel. "The COVID-19 Eviction Crisis: An estimated 30–40 Million People in America Are at Risk." Accessed on April 20, 2021. Https://Nlihc.org/Sites/Default/Files/The_Eviction_Crisis_080720.Pdf.

Fay, Bill. "The US Consumer Debt Crisis." Debt.org. 2019. https://www.debt.org/faqs/americans-in-debt/.

Gallup.com. "Stock Market." April 14, 2020. https://news.gallup.com/poll/1711/stock-market.aspx.

Graeber, David. *DEBT: The First 5,000 Years*. Melville House. 2011.

Kaplan, Jacob. "Jacob Kaplan-Fighting Angiosarcoma, Organized by Jacob Kaplan." Gofundme.com. April 1, 2017. https://www. gofundme.com/f/jacob-kaplanfighting-angiosarcoma.

Konish, Lorie. "137 Million Americans Are Struggling with Medical Debt. Here's What to Know If You Need Some Relief." *CNBC*. November 10, 2019. https://www.cnbc.com/2019/11/10/ americans-are-drowning-in-medical-debt-what-to-know-if-you-need-help.html.

Newyorkfed.org. "The Center for Microeconomic Data—Federal Reserve Bank of New York. 2021. https://www.newyorkfed.org/ microeconomics/hhdc.html.

Rosalsky, Greg. "75 Years Ago the US Dollar Became the World's Currency. Will That Last?" *NPR*. June 30, 2019. https://www.npr. org/sections/money/2019/07/30/746337868/75-years-ago-the-u-s-dollar-became-the-worlds-currency-will-that-last.

Sall, Derek. "The Debt Trap: Selling Yourself into Modern Day Slavery." Life and My Finances. September 23, 2019. https:// lifeandmyfinances.com/2019/09/the-debt-trap-selling-your-self-into-modern-day-slavery/.

Strauss, Ilana E. "The Myth of the Barter Economy." The Atlantic. *The Atlantic*. February 26, 2016. https://www.theatlantic.com/ business/archive/2016/02/barter-society-myth/471051/.

Talks at Google. "Debt: The First 5,000 Years." February 8, 2012. Video, 1:21:09. https://www.youtube.com/watch?v=CZIINXh-GDcs&t=22s&ab_channel=TalksatGoogle

CHAPTER 5

Baker, Anne E. "Getting Short-Changed? The Impact of Outside Money on District Representation." *Social Science Quarterly* 97 (5): 1096–1107. 2016. https://doi.org/10.1111/ssqu.12279.

Blockchains. "Vision in Northern Nevada." Accessed June 7, 2021. https://www.blockchains.com/smart-city/real-life-sandbox/.

Evers-Hillstrom, Karl. "More Money, Less Transparency: A Decade under Citizens United." *OpenSecrets*. January 14, 2020. https://www.opensecrets.org/news/reports/a-decade-under-citizens-united.

FEC.gov. "Sanders, Bernard - Candidate Overview." Accessed on April 20, 2021. https://www.fec.gov/data/candidate/P60007168/.

Hawkings, David. "David Hawkings." LinkedIn. Accessed on April 20, 2021. https://www.linkedin.com/in/davidhawkings/.

Liston, Ryan. "Virginia Becomes 22nd State Supporting Constitutional Amendment Efforts." American Promise. February 3, 2021. https://americanpromise.net/2021/02/virginia-becomes-22nd-state-supporting-constitutional-amendment-efforts/.

Martin, Myles. "Citizens United v. FEC (Supreme Court)." FEC.gov. February 1, 2010. https://www.fec.gov/updates/citizens-united-v-fecsupreme-court/#:~:text=On%20January%2021%2C%20 2010%2C%20othe.

Pew Research Center. "Americans' Views of Government: Low Trust, but Some Positive Performance Ratings." *Pew Research*

Center. September 14, 2020. https://www.pewresearch.org/politics/2020/09/14/americans-views-of-government-low-trust-but-some-positive-performance-ratings/.

Popper, Nathaniel. "A Cryptocurrency Millionaire Wants to Build a Utopia in Nevada." *The New York Times,* November 1, 2018. https://www.nytimes.com/2018/11/01/technology/nevada-Bitcoin-blockchain-society.html.

"Preserving a Strong Democracy." Open.spotify.com. *Money in Politics.* June 2020. https://open.spotify.com/episode/3vPSHUxFy-j3Pj6q7MFNZcZ?si=TaYNgnCnSQyI_gsmFbpTCA.

Pressgrove, Jedd. "Blockchain Voting Debate Heats up after Historic Election." www.govtech.com. November 20, 2020. https://www.govtech.com/products/Blockchain-Voting-Debate-Heats-Up-After-Historic-Election.html.

Schechter, Asher. "Study: Politicians Vote against the Will of Their Constituents 35 Percent of the Time." Pro Market. June 16, 2017. https://promarket.org/2017/06/16/study-politicians-vote-will-constituents-35-percent-time/.

Votem. "Blockchain Voting." Accessed June 7, 2021. https://www.votem.com/blockchain-voting/.

www.presidency.ucsb.edu "Voter Turnout in Presidential Elections—The American Presidency Project." January 22, 2021. https://www.presidency.ucsb.edu/statistics/data/voter-turnout-in-presidential-elections.

CHAPTER 6

Bambrough, Billy. "Elon Musk, the World's Richest Person, Wants to Be Paid in Bitcoin." *Forbes.* January 9, 2021. https://www.forbes.com/sites/billybambrough/2021/01/09/elon-musk-the-worlds-richest-man-wants-to-be-paid-in-Bitcoin/?sh=3f-18beaf433a.

Desjardins, Jeff. "Here's Why Small Businesses Fail." *Business Insider.* August 2, 2017. https://www.businessinsider.com/why-small-businesses-fail-infographic-2017-8?r=US&IR=T.

Entis, Laura. "Where Startup Funding Really Comes from (Infographic)." *Entrepreneur.* November 20, 2013. https://www.entrepreneur.com/article/230011#:~:text=According%20to%20data%20compiled%20by

Horowitz, Andreessen. "Portfolio." Accessed June 7, 2021. https://a16z.com/portfolio/.

Hull, Dana. "Timeline: Elon Musk's Accomplishments." *The Mercury News.* April 10, 2014. https://www.mercurynews.com/2014/04/10/timeline-elon-musks-accomplishments/.

Kennedy, John F. "Inaugural Address." January 20, 1961. https://www.jfklibrary.org/archives/other-resources/john-f-kennedy-speeches/inaugural-address-19610120.

Klebnikov, Sergei. "Elon Musk Is Back at No. 1 Richest Person in the World after Tesla Stock Rebounds." *Forbes.* January 12, 2021. https://www.forbes.com/sites/sergeiklebnikov/2021/01/12/elon-musk-is-back-at-no-1-richest-person-in-the-world-after-tesla-stock-rebounds/?sh=39dc3b056c68.

"Louis Rosenberg." Accessed on April 20, 2021. TEDxKC. https://www.tedxkc.org/louis-rosenberg.

O'Kane, Sean. "Play the PC Game Elon Musk Wrote as a Pre-Teen." *The Verge*. June 9, 2015. https://www.theverge.com/2015/6/9/8752333/elon-musk-blastar-pc-game.

Olivarez-Giles, Nate. "Elon Musk Discusses Tesla and Space X's Near-Bankruptcies during Google Hangout." *The Verge*. August 8, 2013. https://www.theverge.com/2013/8/8/4602772/elon-musk-richard-branson-google-hangout-offers-startup-ceo-advice.

Sba.gov "Grants Programs and Eligibility." Accessed on April 20, 2021. https://www.sba.gov/funding-programs/grants/grants-programs-eligibility.

SEC.gov. "SEC.gov—Cyber Enforcement Actions." June 1, 2021. https://www.sec.gov/spotlight/cybersecurity-enforcement-actions.

Sherry, Benjamin. "What Is an ICO?" *Investopedia*. June 25, 2019. https://www.investopedia.com/news/what-ico/.

Shevchenko, Andrey. "Elon Musk Reveals His True Opinion on Bitcoin and Crypto." *Cointelegraph*. January 24, 2020. https://cointelegraph.com/news/elon-musk-reveals-his-true-opinion-on-Bitcoin-and-crypto.

Strauss, Neil. "Elon Musk: Inventor's Plans for Outer Space, Cars, Finding Love." *Rolling Stone*. November 15, 2017. https://www.

rollingstone.com/culture/culture-features/elon-musk-the-architect-of-tomorrow-120850/.

Unanimous Ai. "Swarm Intelligence Nails Kentucky Derby Superfecta, Turns $20 into $11,000." May 9, 2016. https://unanimous.ai/unu-superfecta-11k/.

CHAPTER 7

Badenhausen, Kurt. "Michael Jordan and 'the Last Dance': By the Numbers." *Forbes*. April 19, 2020. https://www.forbes.com/sites/kurtbadenhausen/2020/04/19/michael-jordan-and-the-last-dance-by-the-numbers/?sh=10c9cc785b15.

Badenhausen, Kurt. "Michael Jordan Has Made over $1 Billion from Nike—The Biggest Endorsement Bargain in Sports." *Forbes*. May 3, 2020. https://www.forbes.com/sites/kurtbadenhausen/2020/05/03/michael-jordans-1-billion-nike-endorsement-is-the-biggest-bargain-in-sports/?sh=4376c6c26136.

Biography. "Taylor Swift." March 15, 2021. https://www.biography.com/musician/taylor-swift.

Cronin, Brian. "When We First Met—When Did Uncle Ben First Say, 'With Great Power Comes Great Responsibility?'" *CBR*. July 15, 2015. https://www.cbr.com/when-we-first-met-when-did-uncle-ben-first-say-with-great-power-comes-great-responsibility/.

Gross, Terry, and Farhad Manjoo. "How 5 Tech Giants Have Become More like Governments than Companies." *NPR*. October 26, 2017. https://www.npr.org/2017/10/26/560136311/

how-5-tech-giants-have-become-more-like-governments-than-companies.

Hehir, Jason. *The Last Dance*. Miniseries. *ESPN*. 2020.

"What Is an Influencer?—Factors That Define a Social Media Influencer." *Influencer Marketing Hub*. January 28, 2021. https://influencermarketinghub.com/what-is-an-influencer/.

"The State of Influencer Marketing 2020: Benchmark Report." *Influencer Marketing Hub*. February 14, 2021. https://influencermarketinghub.com/influencer-marketing-benchmark-report-2020/.

Kelly, Kevin. "The Technium: 1,000 True Fans." Kk.org. March 4, 2008. https://kk.org/thetechnium/1000-true-fans/.

Kettler, Sara. "Marilyn Monroe: Fascinating Facts about the Real Woman behind the Legend." Biography. August 3, 2017. https://www.biography.com/news/marilyn-monroe-biography-facts.

Kulinski, Kyle. "YouTube Cracks down on Controversial Creators." *Secular Talk*. September 1, 2016. Video, 17:18. https://www.youtube.com/watch?v=RW-Dmd4fzZE&ab_channel=SecularTalk.

Marilynmonroe.com. "Marilyn Timeline See All." 2018. https://marilynmonroe.com/about/see-all/.

Mint. "How Much Do YouTubers Make & How to Become a YouTuber." *MintLife* Blog. April 3, 2021. https://mint.intuit.com/blog/relationships/how-much-do-youtubers-make-5035/#:~:-text=With%20the%20average%20YouTube%20pay.

NBA. "Michael Jordan Hall of Fame Class of 2009." Chicago Bulls. NBA.com/bulls. October 6, 2010. https://www.nba.com/bulls/news/jordanhof_2009.html.

Officialdata.org. "$100 in 1971 and 2021—Inflation Calculator." Accessed on April 20, 2021. https://www.officialdata.org/us/inflation/1971?amount=100.

O'Hara, Helen. "How Marilyn Took on Hollywood–and Won." *The Telegraph*, June 1, 2015. https://www.telegraph.co.uk/film/some-like-it-hot/marilyn-monroe-productions-studio/.

Orlowski, Jeff, dir. *The Social Dilemma*. Documentary. Netflix. 2020.

Patreon. "Secular Talk with Kyle Kulinski Is Creating News & Political Commentary." Accessed on April 20, 2021. https://www.patreon.com/seculartalk.

Vaynerchuk, Gary. "My Life & Legacy." GaryVaynerchuk.com. 2017. https://www.garyvaynerchuk.com/my-life-legacy/.

Vaynerchuk, Gary. "Gary Vaynerchuk." GaryVaynerchuk.com. 2021. https://www.garyvaynerchuk.com/biography/.

Western, Dan. "37 Greatest Michael Jordan Quotes of All Time." *Wealthy Gorilla*. https://wealthygorilla.com/22-greatest-michael-jordan-quotes-all-time/.

CHAPTER 8

Bell Team, ed. "'The World Is Your Oyster.'" Bell English. January 15, 2021. https://www.bellenglish.com/blog/world-your-oyster-phrase-week/.

Fontinelle, Amy. "American Debt: Mortgage Debt Reaches $10.04 Trillion." *Investopedia*. February 17, 2021. https://www.investopedia.com/personal-finance/american-debt-mortgage-debt/.

Friedman, Zack. "Student Loan Debt Statistics in 2020: A Record $1.6 Trillion." *Forbes*. February 3, 2020. https://www.forbes.com/sites/zackfriedman/2020/02/03/student-loan-debt-statistics/?sh=31a98c57281f.

Langbridge, James A. *Professional Embedded ARM Development*. Indianapolis: Wrox, A Wiley Brand, 2014.

Roos, Dave. "10 Overrated Life Decisions." *HowStuffWorks*. April 15, 2013. https://money.howstuffworks.com/10-overrated-life-decisions.htm.

CHAPTER 9

Attah, Elikem. "Five Most Prolific 51% Attacks in Crypto: Verge, Ethereum Classic, Bitcoin Gold, Feathercoin, Vertcoin." CryptoSlate. April 24, 2019. https://cryptoslate.com/prolific-51-attacks-crypto-verge-ethereum-classic-Bitcoin-gold-feathercoin-vertcoin/.

Celeb Networth Post. "Charles Ponzi (Criminal): Overview, Biography." Accessed on April 20, 2021. https://www.celebnetworthpost.com/charles-ponzi.

Crypto51.App. "Cost of a 51% Attack for Different Cryptocurrencies." June 2, 2021. https://www.crypto51.app/.

Duignan, Brian. "Donald Trump—Politics" In *Encyclopedia Britannica*. https://www.britannica.com/biography/Donald-Trump.

Encyclopedia.com. "Something Sounds Too Good to Be True, It Probably Is." June 2, 2021. https://www.encyclopedia.com/humanities/dictionaries-thesauruses-pictures-and-press-releases/something-sounds-too-good-be-true-it-probably-if.

Gandhi, Lakshmi. "A History of 'Snake Oil Salesmen.'" *NPR*. August 26, 2013. https://www.npr.org/sections/codeswitch/2013/08/26/215761377/a-history-of-snake-oil-salesmen#:~:text=The%20origins%20of%20snake%20oil.

Edmondson, Brian. "Beware of These Top Bitcoin Scams." *The Balance*. April 14, 2021. https://www.thebalance.com/beware-of-these-Bitcoin-scams-4158112#Bitcoin-scam-1-fake-Bitcoin-exchanges.

Guru99.com. "Potential Security Threats to Your Computer Systems." September 30, 2019. https://www.guru99.com/potential-security-threats-to-your-computer-systems.html.

Hex.com "HEX.COM." Accessed on April 20, 2021. https://hex.com/faq/.

Higgins, Stan. "BitConnect Investors Left in the Lurch as Token's Price Drops 90%." *CoinDesk*. January 17, 2018. https://www.

coindesk.com/bitconnect-investors-left-lurch-tokens-price-drops-90.

Iyengar, Rishi. "Twitter Blames 'Coordinated' Attack on Its Systems for Hack of Joe Biden, Barack Obama, Bill Gates and Others." CNN. July 16, 2020. https://www.cnn.com/2020/07/15/tech/twitter-hack-elon-musk-bill-gates/index.html.

Kessler, Glenn. "Trump Made 30,573 False or Misleading Claims as President. Nearly Half Came in His Final Year." *Washington Post*. January 23, 2021. https://www.washingtonpost.com/politics/how-fact-checker-tracked-trump-claims/2021/01/23/ad04b69a-5c1d-11eb-a976-bad6431e03e2_story.html.

Know Your Phrase. "I Smell a Rat—Meaning, Origin." February 26, 2019. https://knowyourphrase.com/i-smell-a-rat.

Liebkind, Joe. "Beware of These Five Bitcoin Scams." *Investopedia*. September 24, 2020. https://www.investopedia.com/articles/forex/042315/beware-these-five-Bitcoin-scams.asp.

Mix. "How BitConnect Pulled the Biggest Exit Scheme in Cryptocurrency." *The Next Web*. January 17, 2018. https://thenextweb.com/hardfork/2018/01/17/bitconnect-Bitcoin-scam-cryptocurrency/.

Murden, Alastair. "Bernie Madoff Pt.1: Wizard of Wall Street | Con Artists." Spotify. July 2019. https://open.spotify.com/show/6s8x-zsIn1JIvEvoX9sa7sb?si=M9PpFbUUTgCY5u1fycNF0A.

Murden, Alastair. "Charles Ponzi Pt.1: 'the Father of Fraud' | Con Artists." Spotify. April 2020. https://open.spotify.com/

show/6s8xzsIn1JIvEvoX9sa7sb?si=M9PpFbUUTgCY5u-
1fycNFoA.

O'Dea, Simon. "Money Lost to Scam in U.S. 2014-2020." *Statista.*
March 24, 2020. https://www.statista.com/statistics/1050001/
money-lost-to-phone-scam-in-the-united-states/#statisticCo-
ntainer.

Pak, Eudie. "10 Iconic Wild West Figures." *Biography.* April 30,
2020. https://www.biography.com/news/wild-west-figures#:~:-
text=These%20famous%20outlaws%20ruled%20the%20Amer-
ican%20frontier.&text=The%201860s%20and%20the%201890s.

Politifact.com. "PolitiFact." Accessed on April 20, 2021. https://
www.politifact.com/factchecks/list/?speaker=donald-trump.

Quisenberry, William L. "Ponzi of All Ponzis: Critical Analysis of
the Bernie Madoff Scheme." *International Journal of Economet-
rics and Financial Management* 5, no. 1 (2017): 1–6.

Southurst, Jon. "HEX Token Scam Claims Dog Richard Heart's
Scheme." CoinGeek. January 10, 2020. https://coingeek.com/
hex-token-scam-claims-dog-richard-hearts-scheme/.

Wong, Joon Ian. "Every Cryptocurrency's Nightmare Scenario
Is Happening to Bitcoin Gold." *Quartz.* May 24, 2018. https://
qz.com/1287701/Bitcoin-golds-51-attack-is-every-cryptocur-
rencys-nightmare-scenario/.

Zuckoff, Mitchell. Ponzi's Scheme: The True Story of a Financial
Legend. New York: Random House, 2005.

CHAPTER 10

Bitnodes.io. "Global Bitcoin Nodes Distribution." https://bitnodes. io/.

CoinMarketCap. "Ethereum (ETH) Price, Charts, Market Cap, and Other Metrics." June 18, 2021. https://coinmarketcap.com/ currencies/ethereum/.

Cointelegraph Consulting. "Cointelegraph Consulting: Deep Diving with Ethereum Whales." *Cointelegraph*. April 9, 2021. https://cointelegraph.com/news/cointelegraph-consult-ing-deep-diving-with-ethereum-whales.

Cryptopedia Staff. "The DAO: What Was the DAO and How Was It Hacked?" *Gemini*. April 27, 2021. https://www.gemini.com/ cryptopedia/the-dao-hack-makerdao.

Cryptopedia Staff. "Initial Coin Offerings: The Ethereum ICO Boom." *Gemini*. May 27, 2021. https://www.gemini.com/cryp-topedia/initial-coin-offering-explained-ethereum-ico#section-ethereums-role-in-the-ico-boom.

Cussen, Mark. "How to Rebalance Your Portfolio Each Year." *Investopedia*. January 9, 2020. https://www.investopedia.com/ articles/retirement/annual-rebalancing-plan.asp.

Downey, Lucas. "Efficient Market Hypothesis (EMH) Definition." *Investopedia*. March 25, 2021. https://www.investopedia.com/ terms/e/efficientmarkethypothesis.asp.

Egan, Matt. "Worried about a Stock Market Crash? Read This." *CNNMoney*. February 26, 2015. https://money.cnn.

com/2015/02/26/investing/stock-market-crash-bubble-investing/index.html.

Enterprise Ethereum Alliance. "Enterprise Ethereum Alliance." 2021. https://entethalliance.org/.

Ethereum.org. "What Is Ethereum?" 2021. http://ethereum.org.

etherscan.io. "Ethereum Unique Address Growth Chart." Etherscan.io. 2021. https://etherscan.io/chart/address.

Fernando, Jason. "Index Fund." *Investopedia.* February 4, 2021. https://www.investopedia.com/terms/i/indexfund.asp.

Frankenfield, Jake. "Bitcoin Exchange." *Investopedia.* July 13, 2020. https://www.investopedia.com/terms/b/Bitcoin-exchange.asp.

Frankenfield, Jake. "Hot Wallet Definition." *Investopedia.* March 26, 2021. https://www.investopedia.com/terms/h/hot-wallet.asp.

Frankenfield, Jake. "Bitcoin Maximalism." *Investopedia.* May 21, 2021. https://www.investopedia.com/terms/b/Bitcoin-maximalism.asp.

Godbole, Omkar. "Here's a Low-Risk Strategy to Ride the Bull Market CoinDesk." *CoinDesk.* December 1, 2020. https://www.coindesk.com/dollar-cost-averaging-investment-strategy.

Haeberli, Daniel, Stefan Oesterhelt, and Alexander Wherlock. "Blockchain Laws and Regulations—Switzerland." Global Legal Insights International Legal Business Solutions. 2021.

https://www.globallegalinsights.com/practice-areas/block-chain-laws-and-regulations/switzerland.

Hogue, Joseph. "3 Shocking Ways the Stock Market Is Rigged against You." *Stock Market Basics*. June 1, 2020. https://mystockmarketbasics.com/stock-market-rigged/.

Horton, Melissa. "Is It Better to Use Fundamental Analysis, Technical Analysis, or Quantitative Analysis to Evaluate Long-Term Investments?" *Investopedia*. January 23, 2021. https://www.investopedia.com/ask/answers/050515/it-better-use-fundamental-analysis-technical-analysis-or-quantitative-analysis-evaluate-longterm.asp.

Kelleher, John. "Why Do Bitcoins Have Value?" *Investopedia*. March 7, 2021. https://www.investopedia.com/ask/answers/100314/why-do-Bitcoins-have-value.asp.

Land, Kendy. "Open Source Code Development in Cryptocurrency." *Crypt Keepers*. 2020. https://www.cryptkeepers.club/github-data.html.

Land, Kendy. "Ethereum (ETH) Cryptocurrency Evaluation." Crypt Keepers. Accessed on April 20, 2021. https://www.cryptkeepers.club/ethereum-eth.html.

Litman Gregory Investment Team. "Stay the Course: There's a Cost to Timing the Market." Litman Gregory Asset Management. April 28, 2020. https://lgam.com/stay-the-course-theres-a-cost-to-timing-the-market/.

Lynch, Peter. "Bet the Houses." 1995. https://12mv2.files.wordpress.com/2020/09/pl_fortworthcollection.pdf.

Malkiel, Burton G. *Random Walk Down Wall Street: The Time-Tested Strategy for Successful Investing.* W. W. Norton, 2020.

N, Sam. "The Ethereum Team—Founders, Developers & Foundation Members." Blokt: Privacy, Tech, Bitcoin, Blockchain & Cryptocurrency. October 1, 2017. https://blokt.com/guides/team.

Segal, Troy. "Diversification." *Investopedia.* April 21, 2021. https://www.investopedia.com/terms/d/diversification.asp#:~:text=-Diversification%20is%20a%20risk%20management.

Sergeenkov, Andrey. "Who Founded Ethereum?" CoinMarketCap.com. May 12, 2021. https://coinmarketcap.com/alexandria/article/who-founded-ethereum.

CHAPTER 11

Ashford, Kate. "Initial Public Offering: What Is an IPO?" *Forbes Advisor.* February 19, 2021. https://www.forbes.com/advisor/investing/initial-public-offering-what-is-an-ipo/.

Balasubramaniam, Kesavan. "What Are the Advantages and Disadvantages for a Company Going Public?" *Investopedia.* March 18, 2020. https://www.investopedia.com/ask/answers/advantages-disadvantages-company-going-public/.

"Amazon Has Turned a Middle-Class Warehouse Career into a McJob." *South China Morning Post.* December 18, 2020. https://

www.scmp.com/tech/big-tech/article/3114432/amazons-ware-house-pay-rate-has-left-some-workers-homeless-and.

Bragg, Melvyn, Anne Goldgar, Chris Nierstrasz, and Helen Paul. "The Dutch East India Company." *BBC*. March 3, 2016. https://www.bbc.co.uk/programmes/b071vl2l.

Cointelegraph. "ICO vs IPO: Key Differences." Accessed on April 20, 2021. https://cointelegraph.com/ico-101/ico-vs-ipo-key-differences.

DeCambre, Mark. "Coinbase IPO: Everything You Need to Know about the 'Watershed Moment' in Crypto." *MarketWatch*. April 14, 2021. https://www.marketwatch.com/story/coinbase-ipo-everything-you-need-to-know-about-the-watershed-moment-in-crypto-11618350086.

Eos.io. "EOSIO Blockchain Software & Services." Accessed on April 20, 2021. https://eos.io/.

Ghilarducci, Teresa. "Most Americans Don't Have a Real Stake in the Stock Market." *Forbes*. August 31, 2020. https://www.forbes.com/sites/teresaghilarducci/2020/08/31/most-americans-dont-have-a-real-stake-in-the-stock-market/?sh=608862801154.

Gouldman, Daniel. "Ep. 152: Fake Community. Fake Volume. Fake Products. What Is Real in ICO's? W/ Ternio Founders." Spotify. August 2018. https://open.spotify.com/episode/7mMGpuhaJp-KOPXVtAKLK2t.

Hall, Mary. "What 'Going Public' Means." *Investopedia*. September 25, 2020. https://www.investopedia.com/ask/answers/what-does-going-public-mean/.

Hayes, Adam. "Greater Fool Theory." *Investopedia*. May 7, 2021. https://www.investopedia.com/terms/g/greaterfooltheory.asp.

Hudli, Aditi. "Report: Nearly Half of ICOs Failed to Raise Funds since Start of 2017." *CoinDesk*. September 10, 2018. https://www.coindesk.com/report-nearly-half-of-all-icos-fail-to-raise-funds.

Hunters, Ross, and Nadja Picard. "Global IPO Watch—Q4 2020." PwC. March 2021. https://www.pwc.com/gx/en/services/audit-assurance/ipo-centre/global-ipo-watch.html.

ICObench. "EOS (EOS)—ICO Rating and Details." Accessed on April 20, 2021. https://icobench.com/ico/eos.

Investopedia. "BABA." Accessed on April 20, 2021. https://www.investopedia.com/markets/quote?tvwidgetsymbol=baba.

James, Ryan. "'The Biggest IPO in History'—Experts Weigh in on Coinbase IPO." *BeInCrypto*. April 14, 2021. https://bein-crypto.com/the-biggest-ipo-in-history-experts-weigh-in-on-coinbase-ipo/.

Merre, Ruben. "A Comprehensive Guide to the Next Generation of Crypto Funding." Hackernoon.com. February 15, 2019. https://hackernoon.com/a-comprehensive-guide-to-the-next-genera-tion-of-crypto-funding-v-ico-ieo-daico-eto-sto-939909782da6.

Mishel, Lawrence, and Julia Wolfe. "CEO Compensation Has Grown 940% since 1978: Typical Worker Compensation Has Risen Only 12% during That Time." *Economic Policy Institute.* August 14, 2019. https://www.epi.org/publication/ceo-compensation-2018/.

Mulders, Michiel. "List of Best EOS DApps for 2021." Www. youhodler.com. May 12, 2020. https://www.youhodler.com/blog/best-eos-dapps-2020#:~:text=EOS%20blockchain%20is%20a%20decentralized.

Phelan, Ben. "Dutch East India Company: The World's First Multinational." Antiques Roadshow PBS. October 19, 2016. https://www.pbs.org/wgbh/roadshow/stories/articles/2013/1/7/dutch-east-india-company-worlds-first-multinational/.

PricewaterhouseCoopers. "Roadmap for an IPO: A Guide to Going Public." PwC. Accessed on April 20, 2021. https://www.pwc.com/us/en/services/deals/library/roadmap-for-an-ipo-a-guide-to-going-public.html#.

The Investopedia Team. "What Are the Sources of Funding Available for Companies?" *Investopedia.* December 23, 2020. https://www.investopedia.com/ask/answers/03/062003.asp#:~:text=There%20are%20ultimately%20just%20three.

Thomson, Derek. "Considering an IPO to Fuel Your Company's Future?" PwC. 2020. https://www.pwc.com/us/en/services/deals/library/cost-of-an-ipo.html.

Willett, J. R. "Blockchain Only Has One Use Case—J. R. Willett, Inventor of the ICO." Www.youtube.com. September 24, 2018.

Video, 19:47. https://www.youtube.com/watch?v=Nxh4oDLo-a5U&ab_channel=IanBalina.

Zucchi, Kristina. "Top 10 Largest Global IPOs of All Time." *Investopedia*. June 22, 2020. https://www.investopedia.com/articles/investing/011215/top-10-largest-global-ipos-all-time.asp.

CHAPTER 12

Bianchi, Daniele. "Cryptocurrencies: Asset Class or Something Else?" AllAboutAlpha: Alternative Investing Trends and Analysis. October 22, 2020. https://www.allaboutalpha.com/blog/2020/10/22/cryptocurrencies-asset-class-or-something-else/.

Chen, James. "What Is a Reserve Currency?" *Investopedia*. June 13, 2020. https://www.investopedia.com/terms/r/reservecurrency.asp.

Coin Guides. "Satoshi Converter/Calculator—Convert BTC or Satoshi to USD, EUR, AUD." 2021. https://coinguides.org/satoshi-usd-converter/.

Conway, Luke. "The 10 Most Important Cryptocurrencies Other than Bitcoin?" Investopedia. June 1, 2021. https://www.investopedia.com/tech/most-important-cryptocurrencies-other-than-Bitcoin/.

Ganti, Akhilesh. "Asset Class Definition." *Investopedia*. May 22, 2021. https://www.investopedia.com/terms/a/assetclasses.asp.

Macroption.com. "Asset Classes: List, Characteristics, Asset Allocation—Macroption." www. 2021. https://www.macroption. com/asset-classes/#characteristics.

Royal, James, and Kevin Voigt. "What Is Cryptocurrency? Beginners Guide to Digital Cash." *NerdWallet.* June 2, 2021. https://www.nerdwallet.com/article/investing/cryptocurrency-7-things-to-know#:~:text=2.

Ryan, Jake. "Crypto Asset Classes." Hackernoon.com. May 10, 2018. https://hackernoon.com/crypto-asset-classes-6dd6ddece456.

Strickland, Jonathan. "Who Owns the Internet?" *HowStuffWorks.* March 3, 2008. https://computer.howstuffworks.com/internet/ basics/who-owns-internet1.htm.

Tardif, Antoine. "Blockchain Capital's BCAP Token Q4, 2020 Results." Securities.io. January 11, 2021. https://www.securities. io/blockchain-capitals-bcap-token-q4-2020-results/.

Wells, Charlie. "Americans Still Don't Understand How Bitcoin Works." Bloomberg.com, February 19, 2021. https:// www.bloomberg.com/news/articles/2021-02-19/Bitcoin-btc-and-cryptocurrencies-prices-surge-but-understanding-is-limited.

ABOUT THE AUTHOR

———

Ethan Turer is a graduate from California Polytechnic State University, San Luis Obispo, where he studied business entrepreneurship. His intellectual curiosity led him to discover Bitcoin and other cryptocurrencies. He quickly became fascinated with the potential of blockchain technology.

Soon after discovering crypto, Ethan had a big idea for a new kind of cryptocurrency that could change everything. For years, he refined his idea before ultimately writing this book as a way to inspire his readers to help him make Challenge Coin a reality.

Ethan hopes you'll join him on this quest by being a part of the community. Please join *The Next Gold Rush* on Facebook and Discord (and possibly other platforms as well). Also, if you liked what you read and want to support his big idea, you can donate to Ethan Turer through the QR codes/addresses below or Cashapp $EthanTurer. Hopefully, you'll someday be able to invest in Ethan Coin to support his future ventures.

Please send Bitcoin to this address:

bc1qf9zwnh4xxtkg675n0cr4kcerpqadmnhx8jywlq

Please send Ethereum to this address:

0x9aA8dc30c84E9aFD308C34C0e5bb3B508B79498f

Made in the USA
Middletown, DE
04 September 2021

47042091R00146